Sex as a Political Variable

Sex as a Political Variable

Women as Candidates and Voters in U.S. Elections

Richard A. Seltzer
Jody Newman
Melissa Voorhees Leighton

LYNNE RIENNER PUBLISHERS
BOULDER
LONDON

Published in the United States of America in 1997 by
Lynne Rienner Publishers, Inc.
1800 30th Street, Boulder, Colorado 80301

and in the United Kingdom by
Lynne Rienner Publishers, Inc.
3 Henrietta Street, Covent Garden, London WC2E 8LU

Library of Congress Cataloging-in-Publication Data
Seltzer, Richard A.
Sex as a political variable : women as candidates and voters in U.S. elections / Richard A. Seltzer, Jody Newman, Melissa Voorhees Leighton.
Includes bibliographical references and index.
ISBN 1-55587-636-6 (hc : alk. paper)
ISBN 1-55587-736-2 (pbk. : alk. paper)
1. Women in politics—United States. 2. Women politicians—United States. 3. Voting—United States. 4. Sex role—United States. I. Newman, Jody. II. Leighton, Melissa Voorhees, 1969– . III. Title
HQ1236.5.U6S45 1997
306.2'0973—dc21 97-9105
CIP

British Cataloguing in Publication Data
A Cataloguing in Publication record for this book is available from the British Library.

Printed and bound in the United States of America

The paper used in this publication meets the requirements of the American National Standard for Permanence of Paper for Printed Library Materials Z39.48-1984-1984.

5 4 3 2 1

We dedicate this book to our parents, spouses, and children—

Anthony Newman
Bernard and Lillian Seltzer
Charles Leighton
Dan Newman
Florence and Jules Pinsky
Grace Lopes
Michael and Mathew Seltzer
Nancy and Edward Voorhees

Contents

Tables and Figures

Tables

Figures

Acknowledgments

Although we collaborated and worked jointly on all of the material in this book, Richard Seltzer bears primary responsibility for Chapters 2 and 6 and Jody Newman for Chapters 1, 4, and 5. Chapter 3 was a combined effort. Melissa Voorhees Leighton assisted throughout.[1]

Much of the research for Chapters 4 and 5 was done for the National Women's Political Caucus, which has graciously given permission for us to include it here. The National Women's Political Caucus is a national bipartisan nonprofit organization dedicated to increasing the number of elected and appointed women in office at all levels. With state and local chapters across the country and a national headquarters in Washington, D.C., the Caucus recruits, trains, and supports pro-choice women candidates, and does research on women in politics.

The "body" of the book was written in 1995 to 1996. Updates and an epilogue (Chapter 7) were added following the 1996 elections. In general, we felt the results of those elections were in accord with our analysis of previous contests.

We would especially like to thank the following people, who have made invaluable contributions to our research and writing: Harriett Woods, past president of the National Women's Political Caucus, who gave outstanding advice throughout; Jean B. Dugan, who provided excellent editorial and writing advice; Lucy Baruch and the Center for the American Woman and Politics (CAWP) at Rutgers University for invaluable advice and assistance with the study on success rates, including identification and lists of women candidates, and for other excellent data and research they provided; Don Reisman, our editor at Lynne Rienner Publishers, who made many valuable suggestions; William Mayer, of Northeastern University, who provided extremely useful comments in his review;

Clyde Wilcox, of Georgetown University, who also provided many useful comments in his review of our book; Dean Plotnick, Dale Tibbits, Kim Brace, and others at Election Data Services who helped with the gathering and interpretation of state election returns and supervision of data entry; Lee C. Shapiro and others at Voter News Service who provided valuable help by checking some of our results and explaining the details of how their exit polls were conducted; Marilyn Potter and the Roper Center who conducted special computer runs for our analysis; and Michael Asante and Sekou Franklin, who helped gather data and check its accuracy.

We also wish to thank the following people for supplying information, technical assistance, or comments: Eric Austin, Barbara Burrell, Bob Biersack, Margaret Ann Campbell, Susan Carroll, Britt Cocanour, Rhodes Cook, Kent Cooper, Royce Crocker, Robert Darcy, Debra Dodson, Georgia Duerst-Lahti, Jackie Duobinis, Janet Elder, Theresa Esquibel, Bob Faye, Jane Flax, Peter Granda, David Huckabee, Malcolm Jewell, Gary King, Karl Kurtz, Deanna Lee, Susan Lee, Kay LiCausi, Monica McDermit, Joan McLean, Melissa Milstein, Lourdes Sierra, Charles F. Turner, Ron Webber, and Maureen Wener.

Note

1. In an attempt to make this book as readable as possible, we have placed some of the more technical and detailed material in the appendices and have omitted entirely some of the statistical tables upon which the analysis is based. Anyone who wishes copies of those tables should contact Richard Seltzer, Department of Political Science, Howard University, Washington, D.C., 20059.

1

Ten Myths About Women and Politics

Sex and politics have been an explosive combination ever since women won the right to vote. When the League of Women Voters was established in 1919 in the final days of the fight for women's suffrage, the *St. Louis Globe Democrat* wrote that war between the sexes had all but been declared (Mueller, 1988:19). Seventy-five years later, the *Washington Post* echoed the same sentiment in a front page story that claimed: "1996 is shaping up as an unprecedented political war of the sexes in white America" (Edsall, 1995). *U.S. News and World Report* featured a story titled "What Do Women Want?" with a subtitle that is in danger of becoming a cliché: "The Gender Gap Is Now a Chasm" (Borger, 1995). A front page *Wall Street Journal* article (Seib, 1996), which similarly said that the gap appears to be widening into a chasm, compared the political distance between men and women to the interpersonal distance described in the popular book *Men Are from Mars, Women Are from Venus* (Gray, 1992).

The simple, less dramatic truth is that, despite the hype, the gender gap is not a chasm, and there is no war looming between the sexes, at least not in the political arena. Nor is there truth in a lot of other discussion about women and politics that passes as factual. Contrary to popular belief, women candidates don't have a tougher time raising money, nor do they win their races less often than men. Perhaps stemming in part from the current obsession with Mars/Venus differences between the sexes, a great deal of attention is being paid to the gender gap and women in politics, but the subject is often accompanied by misinformation, misunderstanding, and misleading conclusions. In this book we aim to replace the myths and misinformation with facts and reality.

The focus on women and politics is well deserved—not because women are at war with men, nor because they are aliens in their voting behavior, but because women are an overwhelmingly powerful and influential force in elections today. They make up the majority of voters, turn out to vote at higher rates than men, and are formidable candidates, winning as often and raising as much or more money as men in similar races.

In the January 1996 special senate election in Oregon, an astounding 57 percent of voters were women. Men gave a bigger edge to the Republican candidate than women did to the Democrat, but the sheer numbers of women who voted resulted in a victory for Democrat Ron Wyden. In the 1992 presidential election, even though George Bush lost among women, a majority of his voters (53 percent) were women. A force this powerful needs to be well understood and analyzed with sound data and real facts. It is time to debunk the myths and understand the realities that surround women as voters and as candidates.

1. Myth: The gender gap has become a chasm.

Reality: First of all, there clearly *is* a gender gap, or a difference between the way women and men vote. In the 1994 congressional elections the gap was as large as any that have been found since exit polls began reporting votes by sex. However, the gap has not become a chasm, nor does it represent a war between the sexes. To quote Everett Ladd (1996), president of the Roper Center, which collects and archives all national polling data, "This kind of hype is just plain silly."

In 1994, women voted 7 to 11 percentage points more Democratic than men (depending upon which survey you look at), slightly greater than the average gap found in congressional elections over the past decade. Recent polls show a gender gap of 6 to 9 points in head-to-head matchups between Bill Clinton and Bob Dole, the same range as the gaps for George Bush in 1988 and Ronald Reagan in 1984.

Calling the gender gap a chasm can inaccurately depict the gap as a Grand Canyon, with all women on the Democratic side and all men on the Republican side, or give the false impression that most husbands and wives cast their votes for opposing candidates. To explain the gender gap with a simplistic example, imagine a roomful of ten couples. Even with a large gender gap of 10 points, nine of the husbands would be voting the same way as their wives; only one couple would be casting opposing votes.

Focusing narrowly on the gender gap and being obsessed with differences between women and men can obscure the deeper divisions within the U.S. electorate that the gender gap reflects. The parties have become more polarized and ideological, with conservative

Democrats and liberal Republicans rapidly becoming extinct species. In the 1990 congressional elections, about two-fifths of conservatives voted Democratic, while in 1994, less than one-fifth did so.

Any way you slice it, demographic groups are further apart in their voting behavior than they used to be, and the gender gap is not the biggest divide. In 1994, for example, the gap between married and single people was over 12 points; the income gap between rich and poor was 19 points; the gap between urban and rural voters 29 points; and the race gap between whites and blacks was a true chasm of 50 points.

2. Myth: Women didn't go to the polls in 1994, which is why the Republicans took control of Congress.

Reality: The message being promulgated that millions of women who voted in 1992 did not vote in 1994 may be technically true, but it is deceptive. Fewer women voted in 1994 than in 1992, just as fewer men did, because 1992 was a presidential election and 1994 was not. Turnout is always much higher in presidential years. The reality is that women constituted the majority of voters in 1994, just as they have in every election since 1964. Women were no more apathetic in 1994 than in other off-year elections, and they were less apathetic than men.

There has been little change in the share of the electorate that women comprise for the last thirty years. According to national exit polls, women made up 51 percent of the voters in congressional elections in 1994, 50 percent in 1990 (another non-presidential election year), and 52 percent in 1992. The turnout rate for women, which has been higher than the turnout rate for men since 1980, was 44.9 percent of eligible voters in 1994, compared with 44.4 percent for men.

To find differences in the composition of the electorate that may have contributed to Republican victories in 1994, one should look not at sex but at income. People with incomes of $50,000 or higher went from being 11 percent of voters in 1992 to almost one-third of voters in 1994.

3. Myth: The gender gap was born in 1980, fathered by Ronald Reagan.

Reality: National polling data show that there was a gender gap as early as 1952; there is even evidence that women may have voted differently from men ever since they first went to the polls in 1920.

In the 1950s and 1960s, the gender gap reached levels similar to today's (over 9 points in 1956 and over 8 points in 1966), but in those days women, a majority of whom were homemakers, voted more Republican and were more conservative than men.

The gender gap began to be widely discussed in 1980, which is also the year that women began to vote noticeably more Democratic than men. Leaders of women's organizations, picking up on the phenomenon, promoted it in their efforts to pressure legislators to support the Equal Rights Amendment (ERA) and to persuade Walter Mondale to name a woman as his vice-presidential running mate. The National Organization for Women (NOW) put out a monthly "Gender Gap Update," and books on the subject by Eleanor Smeal (1984) and Bella Abzug (1984) were published.

4. Myth: The gender gap grew in 1994 because women were turned off by the Republican message.

Reality: The gender gap grew in 1994 not because women voted more Democratic but because men voted dramatically more Republican. In 1992, 48 percent of men voted Republican in congressional elections; two years later the number grew to 58 percent. Women also voted more Republican in 1994 than in 1992, but by only 2 points.

In fact, women's voting behavior has remained quite stable over the past fifteen years, ranging from 53 to 58 percent Democratic. Men have been more fickle, dropping from 55 percent voting Democratic in 1982 to 42 percent in 1994. The increasing success of the Republican Party, whose members used to be far outnumbered by Democrats, can be explained by the shift in men's partisan loyalties.

5. Myth: The gender gap gives Democratic candidates a big advantage, and Democratic campaigns should do everything they can to make the gap as large as possible.

Reality: A gender gap doesn't give an advantage to anyone. It means only that men and women vote differently, and it does not imply anything about winning or losing an election. When one candidate does better among women than among men, the other candidate does better among men than among women by exactly the same amount. By definition, the Republicans' "problem with women" is exactly the same size as the Democrats' "problem with men."

The increase in the gender gap in 1994 was in fact bad news for Democrats, since it was caused by massive numbers of white men fleeing to the Republican Party. Democrats can win only by gaining the support of even greater numbers of women or by winning back some of the men they lost. Similarly, Republicans can try to woo women their way or continue to strive for further inroads among men.

The term *gender gap,* which is quite different from a lead among women, is often misused and confused. It should be calculated by subtracting the percentage of men who voted for a candidate from the percentage of women who voted for the same candidate (or vice versa). If a candidate had a huge lead among women but an equally huge lead among men, there would be no gender gap at all. Examples of confusion over the term abound. For instance, Bill Clinton's large lead over Dole among women during the 1996 campaign has been cited as evidence of a huge gender gap, but just because Clinton does well among women does not mean there is a gender gap; the gender gap cannot be calculated by looking at women alone. Similarly, the statement made that there was no gender gap in Kathleen Brown's 1994 race for governor of California because she lost among women is not correct; in fact, there was a gender gap, because she lost by even more among men.

A candidate can have a huge gender gap (do much better among women than among men) and yet lose among women. A candidate can also have a huge gender gap, win among women, and yet lose the election. What matters is winning more than 50 percent of voters overall.

None of this is meant to downplay the importance of the gender gap for both parties. A gap of 8 or 9 points can be a huge factor in a close race. As long as Democrats continue to do better among women than among men, they will focus get-out-the-vote efforts on likely Democratic women voters, and Republicans will focus their turnout efforts on men who are likely to vote Republican. But every smart candidate thinks of voters in terms of demographic categories that are much more targeted and specific than "women" or "men."

6. Myth: The gender gap is caused by "women's issues" such as abortion and women's rights.

Reality: The gender gap *is* related to differences on issues, but the issues are not those traditionally called "women's issues," on which men and women tend to agree.

In a nutshell, a higher percentage of women than men have

voted Democratic over the past fifteen years because a smaller percentage of women than men consider themselves conservatives. The chief difference between the sexes on issues is the role of government: A higher percentage of women than men believe in a stronger role for government, particularly on spending for services such as education, health care, and Social Security. In addition, more women than men say they are pessimistic about the performance of the economy, a view that also can be linked to the gender gap in voting.

Men are at least as supportive as women of women's and abortion rights, although women on both sides of the abortion issue are more likely to say they feel strongly about their views. In the January 1996 special election in Oregon, abortion ranked among the top issues of concern to voters; most of those who said it was a top issue voted for the Republican, anti-choice candidate. In general, the issues that are paramount for men in any given election are also paramount for women.

7. Myth: Women form a monolithic voting bloc, commonly known as "the women's vote."

Reality: There is no such thing as "the women's vote." Women are a powerful force in politics today not because they form a voting bloc but because they constitute the majority of voters. Women are a diverse and heterogeneous group of voters, not the special interest group that the term *the women's vote* implies. There are conservative and liberal women, anti-choice and pro-choice, women who oppose affirmative action and those who support it. The answer to the question "What do women want?" depends on which women you ask.

Although the majority (53 percent) of women voted Democratic in 1994, almost half (47 percent) voted Republican; in fact, the majority of white women did vote Republican. Men were a more unified group of voters than women, voting 58 percent Republican and 42 percent Democratic. It makes at least as much sense (or nonsense) to talk of "the men's vote" as "the women's vote."

Savvy politicians approach women voters with the same level of sophistication with which they approach the electorate in general. Women's votes correlate with their race, income level, education, religion, and other demographics, just as men's do. While women's organizations were touting "the women's vote" in the early 1980s, Republicans carefully divided women into sixty-four separate categories, fashioning their strategies and messages accordingly. In the end, Ronald Reagan won not only the 1984 election but also 55 percent of women's votes.

8. Myth: The sex of the candidate makes a big difference to women voters.

Reality: It is often blithely assumed that a woman candidate will attract women voters (for example, a female running mate would have helped Bob Dole win support from women). On the other hand, a number of women candidates, disappointed that women did not all turn out to vote for them, have complained that "women just won't support women."

The truth is that women do tend to vote for women slightly more than men do, although only by a few percentage points. Although women don't automatically vote for women and do not necessarily form a solid base for a woman candidate, the sex of the candidate does affect the gender gap by several points. Our study of exit polls showed that the normal tendency for women to vote for the Democratic candidate grew several points larger when the Democratic candidate was a woman and shrank by several points when the Republican candidate was a woman. Whether this difference arises because a higher number of women will vote for a woman or because a smaller number of men will do so is impossible to determine.

9. Myth: Women, particularly women of color, have a tougher time winning political office than men.

Reality: When similar races are compared, women win as often as men. Electoral success has nothing to do with sex, and everything to do with incumbency.

Our exhaustive study of state and federal elections showed that women's success rates were identical to men's when incumbent women were compared with incumbent men, women running for open seats with men running for open seats, and female challengers with male challengers.

The problem for women candidates is not sex but incumbency. Incumbents, most of whom are men, win much more often than challengers. (U.S. House incumbents win about 95 percent of the time, challengers about 5 percent.) For women to have a level playing field, they have to wait for men to retire, resign, or die, and then run for the open seat.

The chief reason there are so few women in elected office in 1995 (only 10 percent of Congress and just one governor) is that so few women have run. In 1994 women made up only 14 percent of the candidates for the U.S. House, and only 16 percent of all-important open-seat candidates.

Women of color have actually done relatively better than white women. In the U.S. House in 1995, African American women made up 24 percent of African American members; white women made up 9 percent of white members.

10. Myth: Women candidates have a harder time raising money.[1]

Reality: Women candidates raise just as much money as men do when you compare apples with apples—incumbents with incumbents, challengers with challengers, and open seat candidates with open seat candidates. Once again, the problem is not sex but incumbency. A woman challenging an entrenched male incumbent often raises far less money than he does—not because she is a woman but because she is a challenger. Women do have a tougher time in the sense that most incumbents are men, but fund-raising is just as tough for non-incumbent men as for non-incumbent women.

Intensive research has shown that in terms of political action committee (PAC) contributions, large donations, early money, and totals raised, women do at least as well as men in similar situations. In the last several election cycles, in part because of the phenomenal growth of EMILY's List—a PAC that supports Democratic pro-choice women candidates—women have actually been outraising men, particularly in primaries.

* * *

Why is there so much misinformation and mythology surrounding women and politics? Some of the myths have arisen because, in the absence of hard facts and research, political pundits and the press have been forced to rely on conjecture and anecdotal impressions. Other myths were fostered by women candidates themselves who encountered difficulties raising money or winning elections and chose to blame their sex rather than their own abilities or campaigns. Some well-intentioned advocates for women promulgate many of these myths, believing that they are good for women candidates and will increase women's political power.

The raft of press stories in 1995 and 1996 claiming that the gender gap has become a chasm and that women didn't vote in 1994 seem to result from a rare convergence of the interests of the media, pollsters and pundits, and women's organizations. Stories about a war between the sexes and headlines about a record gender gap are colorful and make good copy. Pollsters whose livelihoods depend on finding and tracking new trends can be quoted more often if records are being broken. And groups raising money for women's vote drives believe they will do better if more attention is focused on women voters and women are portrayed as a powerful voting bloc.

But in the end, attempts to promote false perceptions or misleading messages can backfire when the perceptions prove untrue. In the first half of the 1980s, women's organizations devoted a great deal of time and energy to the gender gap, to women's vote drives, and to fostering the idea that women would "elect the next president." They succeeded in selling the gender gap but wound up without the Equal Rights Amendment, with the overwhelming defeat of the first presidential ticket with a woman on it, and with the reelection of Ronald Reagan, a president who had worked against their goals.

In addition, a victim mentality can be damaging to the supposed victims themselves. No one likes to back a sure loser, so the message that women have a tougher time winning elections and a tougher time raising money can only make it more difficult for women to achieve credibility and attract supporters, endorsements, and financial contributions. And if potential women candidates keep hearing how tough conditions will be for them, they will be less likely to decide to run, which will exacerbate the shortage of women candidates, the most severe obstacle to women's political progress today.

Portraying women as a unified voting bloc or as apathetic in the 1994 elections may serve short-term goals, but in the long run, the truth is a much better ally. Often the key to victory, women are a tremendously potent force in elections today, but it is their heterogeneity and the fact that they do turn out to vote that make them so important. Democrats don't stand a chance of winning current elections unless they secure a sizable majority of women's votes, and Republicans, who can win without blacks and without Jews, will be doomed to failure if they don't do well enough among women. Both parties need to woo women precisely because there is not "*a* woman's vote."

The truth is that there is a gender gap. Women do differ from men in their views on the issues and in their voting behavior. But exaggerating this difference, or portraying it as something it is not, will ultimately be damaging to women.

Politics has its own version of urban legends; when conventional wisdom is repeated often enough, perception can become reality. With sex and politics likely to continue as a hot topic, it is important that the myths be separated from political reality. Women voters don't come from another planet, women candidates win as often as men, and, most important, women vote.

Note

1. The subject of women candidates' ability to raise money has been covered so well and thoroughly by Barbara Burrell that it was unnecessary for us to analyze it further for this book. Jody Newman (1984) conducted an early study comparing men's and women's fund-raising in U.S. House races. Newman looked at races from 1976 to 1982 and concluded that by 1982 women were raising as much money as men in comparable races. Barbara Burrell (1994) continued and expanded this research. In *A Woman's Place Is in the House,* Burrell studies the fund-raising of women and men running for the U.S. House of Representatives from 1984 on. Examining each element of fund-raising—total amounts raised and spent, PAC contributions, large donations, and the acquisition of early money—Burrell concludes that "Whether we look at totals, sources or timing, women candidates in similar situations as male candidates generally do as well and sometimes even better in financing their campaigns for national office."

2

How Men and Women Differ on Issues and Demographics

It is clear that on average women and men vote somewhat differently (see Chapter 3). This chapter discusses issues and demographic differences between the sexes that may be the cause of the gender gap in voting.

Analyzing Sex Differences

Our analysis is based on 220 questions from two large-scale academic surveys, the American National Election Studies (NES) and the National Opinion Research Center (NORC).[1] Both NES and NORC[2] choose respondents by using a probability sample of citizens of voting age living in private households. Surveys last one to three hours and are conducted in person.

NES surveys are conducted by the Survey Research Center and the Center for Political Studies of the Institute for Social Research at the University of Michigan, which surveys 1,000 to 2,000 respondents every two years shortly after the elections (Miller, 1994). Historically, NES has been the major source of data used by social scientists to examine voting behavior.

Associated with the University of Chicago, NORC has conducted its General Social Survey (GSS) every year or every other year since 1972 (Davis and Smith, 1992 and 1994), using a sample size of about 1,500. NORC's major goal is to facilitate trend studies in social attitudes. Therefore, NORC pays careful attention to phrasing questions the same way from year to year and asking a large number of questions about political and social attitudes and behavior. NORC's GSS is the survey most often used by social scientists who examine social attitudes and behavior.

Besides calculating the average gap between the responses of men and women for the years in which each of the 220 questions was asked,[3] we studied how the responses varied over time. Whenever we use the term *average gap* (abbreviated as AG), we mean that the difference between men's and women's responses, as well as the general level of agreement or support by both men and women, remained fairly constant over time. If there were important deviations from this average or if the gap grew or shrank over time, we have pointed it out.

Although some NES questions go back to 1952, most of the questions began to be asked in the mid-1970s. We cross-tabulated each question by gender for the years it was asked (about 5,000 cross-tabulations were produced). Chi-square was used to determine statistical significance. This chapter reports only differences and similarities between men and women that are found to be interesting or striking.

We have divided the questions into four broad categories:

- Political Ideology and the Role of Government: These questions examine a person's general orientation toward politics and toward the role of government in domestic and foreign affairs.
- Social Issues: Here we examine specific social issues that are often the subject of political debate.
- Personal Perspectives: These questions concern belief areas that might affect attitudes toward political issues but are rarely the focus of governmental actions.
- Demographic Differences: In this section we examine how men and women differ in the specific conditions of their lives.

Political Ideology and the Role of Government

Women were more likely than men to be liberal in their general political orientation and to favor a stronger role for government and less likely than men to favor an interventionist foreign policy.

Political Ideology. Since the question was first asked in 1972 (see Table 2.1), a consistently higher percentage of men than women have identified themselves as conservatives (AG = 7.8). Women have consistently been more likely than men to say they are moderates (AG = 7.7). The largest gap occurred in 1994, when 53.7 percent of men and 40.0 percent of women identified themselves as conservatives (gap = 13.7). There has been no significant gender gap among those identifying themselves as liberal. In other words, more men than women are conservative; more women than men are moderate; and there is little difference in the percentage who consider themselves liberal.

Table 2.1 Self-Identified Political Views

	Liberal			Moderate			Conservative			
	Male	Female	Gap	Male	Female	Gap	Male	Female	Gap	*p*-value
1972	26.2	25.6	–0.6	36.1	38.5	2.4	37.8	35.9	–1.9	0.0001
1974	27.3	29.1	1.8	32.7	38.9	6.2	40.0	32.0	–8.0	0.0001
1976	27.8	20.8	–7.0	30.5	44.1	13.6	41.8	35.0	–6.8	0.003
1978	26.9	25.9	–1.0	32.6	40.1	7.5	40.5	33.9	–6.6	0.005
1980	25.9	24.8	–1.1	25.7	34.8	9.1	48.4	40.4	–8.0	0.007
1982	19.4	26.3	6.9	33.6	36.2	2.6	47.1	37.5	–9.6	0.005
1984	25.9	25.3	–0.6	29.6	37.0	7.4	44.5	37.7	–6.8	0.0001
1986	23.9	23.4	–0.5	30.9	41.9	11.0	45.1	34.7	–10.4	0.003
1988	24.7	22.2	–2.5	26.8	35.3	8.5	48.6	42.5	–6.1	0.002
1990	26.1	23.7	–2.4	31.8	41.0	9.2	42.0	35.2	–6.8	0.001
1992	25.8	29.4	3.6	29.1	33.9	4.8	45.1	36.7	–8.4	0.0001
1994	17.8	21.8	4.0	28.5	38.2	9.7	53.7	40.0	–13.7	0.0001

NES asked respondents to rank a variety of political players on a 0–100 "feeling thermometer."[4] In general, relative to women, men have had more negative attitudes toward the Democratic Party (AG = 7.3), toward Democratic presidential candidates (AG = 5.6), toward Democratic congressional candidates (AG = 3.8), and toward liberals (AG = 8.5).

On the other hand, men and women differ less in their attitudes toward Republicans and conservatives.[5] There is a much larger gap in men's and women's attitudes toward Democrats and liberals than toward Republicans and conservatives.

Government's Role in Solving Societal Problems. Women were more likely than men to want a greater role for government in social services and to support policies that help the disadvantaged.[6] For example, more women than men said the government should be spending more on Social Security (AG = 8.9 since 1984).

Women were more likely than men to believe government should play a more activist role in the following areas: "improving the standard of living of all poor Americans" (AG = 8.8), "seeing to it that every person has a job and a good standard of living" (AG = 6.6 since 1972), "doing even more to solve the country's problems" rather than leaving matters to individuals and private businesses (AG = 10.1), and providing "more services in areas such as health and education . . . even if it means an increase in spending" (AG = 12.2).[7]

Women were somewhat more likely than men to say that spending was too little or about right on health, welfare, education, and big-city problems. They also were somewhat more likely than men to think that government should be concerned with reducing income differences between the rich and the poor, helping people pay for medical care, and developing a government health insurance plan.[8] However, none of these gaps averaged more than 5 points.

On the other hand, men were more likely than women to say spending was too little on areas related to infrastructure: parks and recreation (AG = 3.7), mass transportation (AG = 5.4), highways and bridges (AG = 7.4), and space exploration (AG = 16.7). There was virtually no gender difference on support for the amount of money spent on improving and protecting the environment, the overall support having stayed about the same since 1972.

Defense and Foreign Policy. The data on defense and foreign policy are contradictory. Men have expressed somewhat greater confidence than women in the military (AG = 4.5), but it is unclear if that confidence translates into increased support for defense spending. NORC data showed women somewhat more likely than men to say that defense spending was either too little or about right (AG = 2.7 since 1973), whereas NES data showed women advocating somewhat greater cuts than men in defense spending (AG = 3.3 since 1980).

Women have been more critical of communism than men. Until 1994, women were on average 10 points more likely than men to say that communism was the "worst kind of government." Interestingly, in 1994 this gap dropped to 2.9 points.

However, this anti-communist sentiment did not translate into a desire for the United States to become more involved in world affairs. Since the 1950s, women have consistently been more likely than men to believe that "this country would be better off if it . . . did not concern itself with problems in other parts of the world" (AG = 6.2). Men and women generally have held similar views on foreign aid.

There have not been many long-term questions from NORC or NES relevant to foreign policy.[9] To rectify this deficiency, we examined the 1994 national survey sponsored by the Chicago Council on Foreign Relations (CCFR). Three conclusions can be drawn from our analysis of the CCFR data:

1. Women are more likely than men to state they have no opinion about many of the questions asked. For example, 20.4 percent of women and 9.9 percent of men said they were unsure whether or not the United States had a vital interest in the Middle East. We found differences in "don't know" rates of 10 percent or more in 14 of the 110 questions we examined. It is unclear whether these differences occur because women have less knowledge of foreign affairs than men, because women are less likely than men to venture opinions on

areas they don't feel strongly about, or because men are less willing than women to admit they don't know the facts.

2. Men and women see somewhat different goals for U.S. foreign policy. Men were more likely than women to say the following goals were very important: protecting weaker nations against foreign aggression (28.3% v. 21.3%), promoting and defending human rights (37.6% v. 32.6%), reducing the trade deficit (64.6% v. 58.3%), maintaining superior military power (55.1% v. 47.0%), and defending the security of our allies (45.6% v. 39.8%). Women were more likely than men to mention the following goals as very important: combating world hunger (61.9% v. 51.2%), strengthening the UN (56.2% v. 49.9%), improving the global environment (62.4% v. 56.2%), and stopping the flow of illegal drugs into the United States (88.9% v. 81.6%). Some of these differences between men and women mirror those we see in attitudes toward domestic issues.

3. Men were more likely than women to favor the United States taking "an active part in world affairs" (74.4% v. 63.6%). The largest differences in the survey were found in support for using U.S. troops. Men were far more likely than women to support using troops if North Korea invaded South Korea (49.1% v. 29.7%), Iraq invaded Saudi Arabia (62.0% v. 42.6%), Arab forces invaded Israel (47.0% v. 37.8%), or Russia invaded Western Europe (61.4% v. 46.7%).

Social Issues

Although there were exceptions, we found that women were somewhat more likely than men to be liberal on issues of racial politics and criminal justice. However, women were more likely than men to exhibit conservative opinions about sexual freedoms and civil liberties for controversial groups. Contrary to popular wisdom, we found few differences between men and women on what have commonly been called "women's issues." Men were generally more optimistic about the economy than women.

Racial Attitudes. A higher percentage of women than men expressed positive feelings toward blacks (AG = 8.9).[10] Women were somewhat more liberal than men on government programs that directly benefit blacks.

Women were more likely than men to attribute differences between blacks and whites in jobs, income, and housing to racial discrimination (AG = 5.4) and fewer educational opportunities for blacks (AG = 4.5).[11] Women were somewhat more likely than men to say that government is spending too little money on "improving the conditions of blacks," that it should give special treatment to blacks to make up for past discrimination, and that it should make "every possible effort to improve the social and economic position of blacks." None of these gaps averaged more than 6 points.

On the other hand, women were somewhat more likely than men to say there should be laws against interracial marriage (AG = 1.6), and there were few differences between men and women on whether whites "have a right to keep blacks out of their neighborhoods."

Gender Politics. There were few differences between men and women on so-called women's issues such as abortion and equality for women.[12] We did find, however, some gender differences on support for the Equal Rights Amendment (ERA) the women's movement, and related children's issues.

Reproductive Rights. Although this issue has been strongly identified with the women's movement,[13] in general, men and women have had a similar level of support for abortion rights since 1972.[14] But in almost every instance where there was a statistically significant gender gap, men were slightly more likely than women to support a woman's right to abortion.[15]

NORC asked respondents in 1982 and 1984 how strongly they held their attitudes toward abortion. In 1984 women were more likely than men to say they were very "personally concerned about the abortion issue" (38.1% of women v. 23.2% of men; gap = 14.9); to say they were very unlikely to change their opinion about abortion (64.7% v. 53.6%; gap = 11.1); and to say that abortion was an important issue to them (68.1% v. 56.0%; gap = 12.1).[16]

The Role of Women. Both men and women increasingly agree that women should have an equal role in society.[17] Table 2.2 shows that since the early 1970s there has been a large and consistent increase in support for women's equality among both sexes and the differences between men and women on these issues have been fairly small.

An interesting exception to the similarity between men and women on these issues appeared in the responses to whether "women should have an equal role with men in running business, industry and government . . . [or whether] women's place is in the home." Men were slightly more likely than women to choose "an equal role" in almost every year (AG = 3.3). In 1994, 74.7 percent of men and 68.6 percent of women advocated an equal role for women (gap = 6.1).

The Equal Rights Amendment. Men and women had very similar attitudes toward the ERA when they were questioned by NORC in 1977. In 1982, women were somewhat more likely than men to support the ERA (gap = 4.2) but more likely to say the issue was important to them (57.4% of women v. 47.4% of men; gap = 10.0).

Table 2.2 Attitudes Toward the Role of Women: Changes over Time and Differences Between Men and Women

	Men and Women Combined (% agree)		Men and Women Compared (1994) (% agree)	
	First Asked	1994	Men	Women
Most men are better suited emotionally for politics than are most women. (First asked in 1974.)	47.0%	20.9%	21.7%	20.4%
If your party nominated a woman for president, would you vote for her if she were qualified for the job? (1972)	73.6%	92.0%	91.5%	92.3%
Women should take care of running their homes and leave running the country up to men. (1974)	35.6%	14.1%	14.6%	13.8%
It is much better for everyone involved if the man is the achiever outside the home and the woman takes care of the home and family. (1977)	65.8%	35.0%	38.4%	32.7%
It is more important for a wife to help her husband's career than to have one herself. (1977)	57.1%	21.6%	22.2%	21.1%
Recently there has been a lot of talk about women's rights. Some people feel that women should have an equal role with men in running business, industry, and government. Others feel that women's place is in the home. Where would you place yourself on this scale or haven't you thought much about this? (1972, Percentage responding 1, 2, or 3 on a 7-point scale, with 1 representing most in favor of equal role for women)	48.9%	71.5%	74.7%	68.6%

The Women's Movement. There has been a dramatic increase in support for the women's liberation movement among both men and women since NES first asked about it in 1970. The level of positive sentiment increased from 18.1 percent in 1970 to 60.7 percent in 1994. Women have averaged higher support for the women's movement than men over the ten years the question was asked (AG = 5.5). This gap has been growing over time and was at its highest in 1994 (65.3% v. 55.8%; gap = 9.5).

Children's Issues. Both men and women are becoming somewhat less likely to say that the young children of women are hurt when women work. For example, the proportion of respondents who agreed that "a preschool child is likely to suffer if his or her mother works" declined from 67.3 percent in 1977 to 42.5 percent in 1994. However, there was a large gender gap every year this question was asked. For this and a related NORC question, men were consistently more likely than women to believe that children suffer when mothers work (50.6% of men v. 36.8% of women in 1994; gap = 13.8).

In 1990 women were slightly more likely than men to support increases in government spending for children's programs such as child care, Head Start, and school lunches.[18] A more discernible gap occurred in 1994 on two related questions. Women were more likely than men to agree strongly that "working women should receive maternity leave when they have a baby" (32.9% of women v. 22.5% of men; gap = 10.4) and that "families should receive financial benefits for child care when both parents work" (18.7% v. 10.5%; gap = 8.2).

Sexual Freedoms. Women were generally more conservative than men on issues related to sexual freedoms.

Women were much more likely to agree that "there should be laws forbidding the distribution of pornography" (AG = 17.9) and were more likely than men to believe that pornography leads to rape and a breakdown of morals.

Men were less likely than women to view premarital or extramarital sex as wrong (see Table 2.3). The gap averaged 11.9 points on premarital sex and 7.2 points on extramarital sex.

There were few or no differences between men's and women's views on homosexuality, sex education in the schools, birth control for teenagers, and divorce laws.

Society as a whole has become more tolerant on some of these issues, with fewer men and women in the 1990s than in the 1970s saying that premarital sex and homosexuality are wrong. As shown in Table 2.3, views on premarital sex have shifted approximately 12 percentage points since the early 1970s. Attitudes toward pornography, divorce laws, sex education, and making birth control available to teenagers have remained fairly constant. In the area of extramarital sex, society has become somewhat more conservative.

Civil Liberties. NORC asked respondents about their views on civil liberty guarantees for five controversial groups (homosexuals, atheists, communists, militarists, and racists). Respondents were asked whether people in each of the groups should be allowed to make public speeches or teach at a college or university and whether their books should be removed from the public library.[19]

Women were consistently less likely than men to support civil liberties for atheists, racists, and communists. For example, in 1994 men were more likely than women to support the speaking rights of atheists (75.8% of men v. 71.9% of women; gap = 3.9), racists (66.7% v. 59.3%; gap = 7.4), and communists (73.1% v. 64.3%; gap = 8.8).

Table 2.3 Attitudes Toward Sexual Freedoms: Changes Over Time and Differences Between Men and Women

	Men and Women Combined (% always wrong or almost always wrong)		Men and Women Compared (1994) (% always wrong or almost always wrong)		
	First Asked	1994	Men	Women	Gap
If a man and a woman have sexual relations before marriage, do you think it is always wrong, almost always wrong, wrong only sometimes, or not wrong at all? (first asked 1972)	48.5%	36.1%	28.3%	41.5%	13.2
What about sexual relations between two adults of the same sex—do you think it is always wrong, almost always wrong, wrong only sometimes, or not wrong at all? (1973)	81.0%	70.5%	73.1%	68.5%	4.6
What is your opinion about a married person having sexual relations with someone other than the marriage partner—is it always wrong, almost always wrong, wrong only sometimes, or not wrong at all? (1973)	69.6%	78.5%	81.0%	75.3%	5.7

This may be related to the fact that women have been more likely than men to express views that are religious, anti-racist, and anti-communist. There were almost no gender differences on questions regarding militarists or homosexuals.

Crime and Legal Issues. As might be expected, women have been far more likely than men to fear walking alone at night. The gap between men and women has averaged 36.8 points since 1973 (60.5% of women v. 30.3% of men in 1994; gap = 30.2).

Men have been more likely than women to say they have been a victim of crime.[20] Since 1973 men have been far more likely than women to say they have been "threatened with a gun, or shot at" (AG = 21.5).[21]

On some issues, women were more likely than men to support a "law and order" perspective. Women were somewhat more likely than men to say the courts were not harsh enough in dealing with criminals (AG = 2.5), more likely to oppose the legalization of marijuana (AG = 8.0 since 1973), and more likely to favor requiring permits for a gun purchase (AG = 14.7). In addition, women were somewhat more likely than men to support increased spending on drug addiction (AG = 3.4) and crime (AG = 5.4). However, men have been more likely to support capital punishment (AG = 9.0) and to say they have a gun in their house (AG = 14.0).

The Economy. Men were more positive than women about the performance of the economy over the previous year (AG = 7.5) and about whether their family was better off financially than a year ago (AG = 6.3). Men were also somewhat more optimistic about the prospects for improvements in the economy (AG = 3.2) and their family finances (AG = 6.3) over the coming year, but there was little difference between men and women in their estimation of the chances that their family finances would get worse (AG = 0.3).

Personal Perspectives

There were inconsistent differences between men and women in terms of their personal satisfaction and levels of alienation. Women were more likely than men to be religious and men were somewhat more likely than women to participate in organizations.

Personal Satisfaction. Men were more likely than women to say they found life to be exciting (AG = 6.3). They also expressed somewhat greater satisfaction than women with their marriages (AG = 3.6 since 1973)[22] and their health and physical condition (AG = 4.2).

Women were more likely than men to express satisfaction with their friendships (AG = 6.0) and somewhat more likely than men to be satisfied with their family life (AG = 3.6 since 1973). They also were somewhat more likely than men to be satisfied with where they live (AG = 3.6).

There was little difference between men and women in general happiness or in terms of satisfaction with their jobs. However, when asked what they most preferred about a job, women were somewhat more likely to mention feelings of accomplishment and men were somewhat more likely to mention high income and job security.[23]

Alienation. Two types of alienation were studied for gender differences: (1) political alienation, or the extent to which men and women mistrust their government, and (2) interpersonal alienation, or the extent to which men and women mistrust one another or have little hope in the future.

Political Alienation. One of the defining elements of modern U.S. politics is the increased extent to which citizens no longer trust the government.[24] NORC found a dramatic increase between 1973 and

1994 in the proportion of the population expressing little confidence in Congress (15.3% in 1973 vs. 40.5% in 1994) and in the executive branch (18.7% in 1973 and 35.7% in 1994). NES data show that between 1958 and 1994 the proportion of the population that said they "can trust the government in Washington to do what is right . . . only some of the time" jumped from 24.3 percent to 78.9 percent.

On most questions of political alienation, women and men had similar views. The following are some exceptions:

- Men were more likely than women to say they have hardly any confidence in Congress (AG = 5.6 since 1972) and to believe that government wastes a lot of our tax dollars (AG = 5.2 since 1964).
- A higher proportion of men had confidence in the U.S. Supreme Court (AG = 6.0).
- Women were more likely than men to believe that government is too complicated (AG = 13.4 since 1952).[25]
- Women were somewhat more likely than men to believe that most officials are crooked (AG = 4.0 since 1958).

Interpersonal Alienation. In the general population there has been a decline in the proportion of people who say they can trust others (47.9% in 1972 v. 35.7% in 1994; change = 12.2), with women being generally less trustful than men.

Women were more likely than men to believe that the "lot of the average man is getting worse" (AG = 5.9 since 1973) and that "it's hardly fair to bring a child into the world with the way things look for the future" (AG = 4.4 since 1973). Women were somewhat more likely to believe that "you can't be too careful in dealing with people" (AG = 4.7 since 1972).

On the other hand, women were more likely than men to believe that "most of the time people try to be helpful" (AG = 7.8 since 1972) and that most people try to be fair (AG = 4.2 since 1972). Women were somewhat more likely to say people got ahead by their own hard work, while men were more likely to credit lucky breaks.

Religion. Many conservative fundamentalist religious organizations identify with the Republican Party and there is a tendency for religious people to vote Republican.[26] In light of the fact that women have tended to vote more Democratic since 1980, it is interesting to find that women have been far more likely than men to say they are religious. Women averaged more than 10 points higher than men on each of four indicators of religiosity: strength of religious affiliation, frequency of church attendance, membership in a church-affiliated group, and belief in the Bible as God's word.[27] Women have had only slightly more confidence than men in the people running organized religious institutions (AG = 2.7).

Participation in Politics and Society. *Political Participation.*[28] In general, women and men claimed to have similar levels of political participation. Women were less likely than men to know the names of congressional candidates in their district (AG = 7.6), less likely to say they had attempted to influence the vote of another person (AG = 9.2), and somewhat less likely to say they had donated money to a candidate (AG = 2.8).

Organizational Participation. Men were more likely than women to say they participated in organizations. For example, in 1994, 75.8 percent of men and 64.5 percent of women said they were members of at least one organization (gap = 11.3). Men have been more likely than women to say they were members of a labor union (AG = 12.9), a fraternal group (AG = 8.1), veteran's group (AG = 8.8), or sports club (AG = 12.5). Women were more likely than men to join school service organizations (AG = 6.7) and literary, art, discussion, or study groups (AG = 3.7). There were few differences between men and women concerning membership in nationality groups, school fraternities, hobby clubs, service clubs, political clubs, or youth groups.

Leisure Time. Women were more likely than men to say they spent a social evening once a month or more with a brother or sister (AG = 6.3), a parent (AG = 4.8), or relatives (AG = 6.4). There were no substantial differences between men and women in the amount of time they said they spent with friends or neighbors.

Women were more likely to say they watched television at least three hours a day (AG = 5.1), and men were more likely to say they read a daily newspaper (AG = 5.3).

Men were more likely than women to say they went to a bar at least once a month (AG = 14.0) and drank alcoholic beverages (AG = 11.6). Until 1994, men were more likely than women to say they smoked cigarettes. The gap in smoking has been steadily decreasing.

Demographic Differences

One of the most remarkable social changes that has occurred over the past forty years is the movement of women from the household to the labor force. In 1952 over two-thirds of women were homemakers; in 1994 less than one-fifth were. Women have caught up with men in terms of educational attainment, and there has been progress in the area of income, but women are still being paid less than men who have comparable levels of education. In addition, women are still far more likely than men to occupy sales and clerical jobs.

Income. The difference in income between men and women has narrowed since the 1970s. However, the gap is still substantial and is greater among those with less education.

It is difficult to obtain accurate yearly historical data on income differentials between men and women. The best recent data on this issue is found in Bernstein (1995), from which Tables 2.4 and 2.5 are adapted.[29] In Table 2.4 hourly wages for males and females in 1973 and 1993 are displayed by race for differing levels of education.[30] In 1973, white women earned on average 63.9 percent of the income of white men and black women earned 78.5 percent of the income of black men. By 1993, these proportions had changed to 76.3 percent and 90.9 percent, respectively. Progress has been made, but even after controlling for education, race, and the hours worked, substantial income differences still exist.[31]

Table 2.4 Hourly Earnings, by Sex and Race, Ages 18–64 (1993 Dollars)

	Less Than High School	High School	Some College	College	College 2+ Yrs
Whites					
1973 Male	$12.25	$13.93	$14.48	$19.41	$21.37
1973 Female	$7.35	$8.82	$9.83	$12.80	$16.90
M/F Proportion	60.0%	63.3%	67.9%	65.9%	79.1%
1993 Male	$9.45	$11.59	$13.09	$17.88	$22.01
1993 Female	$6.78	$8.71	$10.34	$13.59	$17.63
M/F Proportion	71.7%	75.2%	79.0%	76.0%	80.1%
Blacks					
1973 Male	$9.83	$11.08	$12.22	$14.66	na
1973 Female	$6.80	$8.27	$10.16	$14.79	na
M/F Proportion	69.2%	74.6%	83.1%	100.9%	
1993 Male	$8.15	$9.21	$10.72	$15.00	$17.31
1993 Female	$6.64	$7.99	$9.60	$13.48	$17.71
M/F Proportion	81.5%	86.8%	89.6%	89.9%	102.3%

Source: Adapted from Jared Bernstein, *Where's the Payoff? The Gap Between Black Academic Progress and Economic Gains*, Economic Policy Institute, 1995, Table E.

Education. According to Bernstein's data on the educational attainment of men and women (see Table 2.5), men had greater levels of education than women in 1975.[32] Among whites in particular, men were more likely than women to have graduated from college (27.3%

Table 2.5 Educational Attainment, by Sex and Race, Ages 25–34

	Less Than High School	High School	Some College	College+
Whites				
1975 Male	14.7%	37.2%	20.9%	27.3%
1975 Female	16.1	47.5	17.3	19.1
1990 Male	10.1%	42.1%	21.1%	26.7%
1990 Female	8.5	41.7	23.9	25.9
Blacks				
1975 Male	30.1%	41.8%	17.5%	10.6%
1975 Female	31.7	44.2	14.4	9.8
1990 Male	17.0%	47.4%	21.8%	13.9%
1990 Female	17.3	44.6	24.8	13.3

Source: Adapted from Jared Bernstein, *Where's the Payoff? The Gap Between Black Academic Progress and Economic Gains*, Economic Policy Institute, 1995, Table A.

of men v. 19.1% of women). By 1990 these educational differences were minimal.

Employment Status. There has been a dramatic increase in the proportion of women in the labor force in the last four decades (see Figure 2.1). In 1952, 65 percent of women were homemakers, compared with 18.2 percent in 1994. The proportion of women in 1994 who were employed (56.6%) continued to lag behind the proportion of men who were employed (73.4%), but the gap has steadily declined, from a high of 58.8 in 1952 to a low of 16.8 in 1994.[33]

Occupation. Because of comparability problems across years, NES grouped people into three broad occupational categories (for example, all professional and managerial occupations were combined). Within each of these categories, the gap between men and women has been remarkably consistent over the last forty years. There has been only a small difference between men and women who were in the professional/managerial category (AG = 4.5 over 42 years). In 1994, 33.3 percent of men and 28.0 percent of women were professionals or managers. The gaps in the two other categories were much larger. For clerical/sales jobs, the gap averaged 23.1 points; in 1994, 16.6 percent of men were in these positions, compared with 40.5 percent of women. For blue-collar occupations, the gap has averaged 18.6 points, with 50.1 percent of men and 31.5 percent of women holding these jobs in 1994. Clearly, relative to men, women have been and continue to be far less likely to have blue-collar

Figure 2.1 Women's Employment Status, 1952–1994 (Percentage Employed)

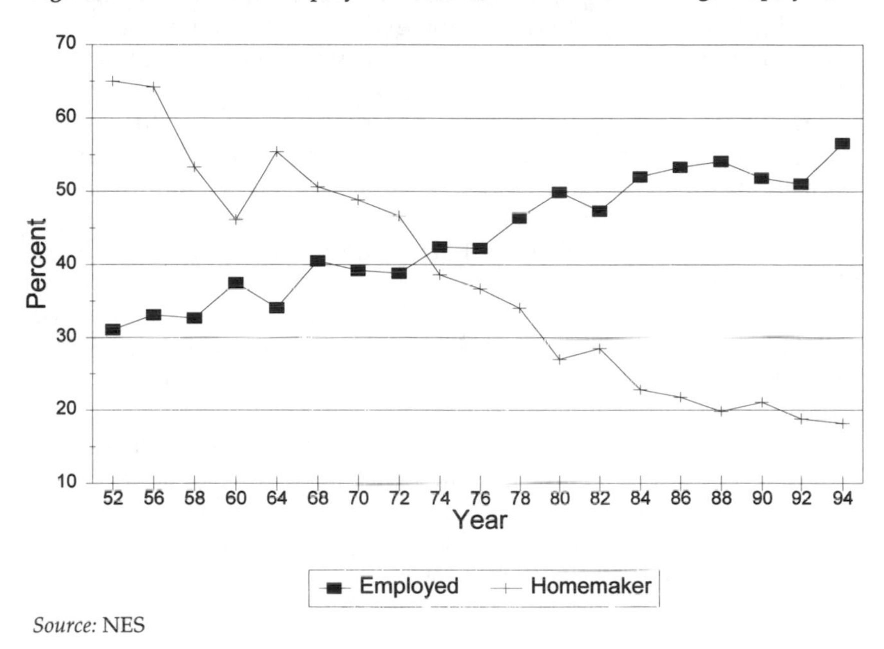

Source: NES

occupations, somewhat less likely to hold professional/managerial occupations,[34] and far more likely to be in clerical or sales occupations.

Marriage. Men have been far more likely than women to be married (AG = 13.4) and somewhat more likely to have never married (AG = 3.1). Women have been far more likely than men to be widowed (AG = 11.9) and somewhat more likely to be divorced or separated (AG = 4.6). These differences in marital status have remained fairly constant since 1956.

Conclusions[35]

We found five areas in which significant gender differences might make women more likely than men to vote Democratic: political ideology, spending on social services, racial attitudes, faith in the economy, and demographic differences. Women were less likely than men to label themselves as conservatives and to be optimistic about the economy. Women were more likely than men to favor governmental actions to help the disadvantaged and to be demographically situated such that they would benefit from governmental actions that would improve the lives of the disadvantaged.

However, there were three areas in which gender differences might make women more conservative and more likely than men to vote Republican: sexual freedoms, civil liberties, and religion. Women were more likely than men to hold conservative positions on sexual mores and civil liberties. Furthermore, women were far more likely than men to be religious.

In six areas differences between men and women were small or inconsistent: gender politics, satisfaction levels, political and organizational participation, alienation, foreign policy, and criminal justice issues.[36]

Although we have focused on areas in which men and women differed, similarities between women and men outweighed their differences. Contradictions, inconsistencies, and lack of differences were more often the rule than the exception. Women and men are not monolithic in their views on issues.

Notes

1. A series of indices from these questions (i.e., one index on abortion, another on racial attitudes, and so on) was not created for three reasons:

- Some questions were not asked in every year. Therefore, it was not possible to create uniform indices over time.
- The logic for which questions to include in the indices changed over time. For example, in the 1960s it might have made theoretical sense to combine questions on pornography and premarital sex into an index on sexual freedom. However, this logic would no longer be valid in the 1990s.
- Combining questions could lose important differences among the questions. One might combine attitudes toward homosexuality and premarital sex into an index on sexual freedom, but the gender difference on these two questions is not parallel and information would be lost by combining them.

2. For a more detailed discussion of the data sources, see Appendix 1.

3. We attempt to be consistent in labeling gaps. In particular, gaps under 5 points are considered small, while gaps over 10 points are considered more substantial.

4. Respondents were asked to rate political players on a 0 to 100 scale where 0 meant they felt very unfavorable and 100 meant very favorable. Analyzed were NES thermometer questions about the presidential candidates (first asked in 1968), congressional candidates (1978), members of the political parties, and liberals and conservatives (1964). These scales were

collapsed into three categories (negative: 0–40; neutral: 41–60; and positive: 61–100).

5. The negative rating gaps between men and women were small on attitudes toward the Republican Party (AG = 0.1), the Republican presidential candidates (0.7), and Republican congressional candidates (–1.3). Women were somewhat more positive than men toward Republican congressional candidates (AG = 3.9). Men were both more positive (–2.8) and more negative (–2.4) than women toward conservatives.

6. In other related questions, women were somewhat more positive than men toward poor people (AG = 4.2) and people on welfare (AG = 6.4)

7. Most of these questions were phrased in a way that pitted the role of government versus the responsibility of individuals. For example, "Some people think that the government in Washington is trying to do too many things that should be left to individuals and private businesses. Others disagree and think that the government should do even more to solve the country's problems." Respondents were then asked to choose one of these positions or to put themselves somewhere in the middle.

8. In 1994 women were far more likely than men to support the position that it is the government's responsibility "to see to it that people have help in paying for doctors and hospital bills" versus the position that "people should take care of these things themselves" (84.7% v. 72.5%; gap = 12.2). This sudden increase in the gap occurred because male support for a greater government role dropped by 10 points since 1992 and may have been influenced by the debate over Clinton's health care proposals.

9. In part, this is because the world and important foreign policy issues change over time. For example, questions about sending U.S. troops to Vietnam are not relevant in the 1990s and questions about Bosnia would not have been asked in the 1970s. Therefore, questions relative to foreign policy have been more general in nature.

10. In 1994, 63.1 percent of women and 52.5 percent of men expressed a positive attitude toward blacks (gap = 10.6). It is interesting that the most abstract racial question generated the largest gap. Clearly, abstract support does not necessarily lead to support for concrete measures to alleviate problems of discrimination. See Jackman (1981) for more on this element of abstract support.

11. In recent years the gap between men and women has grown larger in two areas related to racial attitudes:

- Only since 1992 have women been more likely than men to say the government should "see to it that white and black children go to the same schools" (49.1% of women v. 37.9% of men in 1994; gap = 11.2).
- Before 1985, NORC found that men were slightly more likely than women to believe that "blacks shouldn't push themselves where they're not wanted" (AG = 3.8). When NORC asked this question again in 1994, the gender gap was far larger (49.9% of men v. 39.7% of women; gap = 10.2).

12. There has been disagreement among other analysts on this issue. Shapiro and Mahajan (1986) examined questions from a variety of survey organizations and found that women were more conservative than men on women's rights issues. Deitch (1988) and Simon and Landis (1989) examined

a number of polls and found few differences between men and women in areas of gender politics. However, Conover (1988) examined data from the 1985 NES Pilot Study and found that women who had a strong feminist identity (strongly affected by age) were considerably more liberal than men and other women and concluded that there was a distinctive women's perspective characterized by an ethic of caring. Cook and Wilcox (1991) critiqued Conover's analysis when they analyzed similar 1984 data from NES. They noted that "feminist" men were as liberal as "feminist" women and that the values and policy preferences associated with feminism are not uniquely feminine.

13. However, previous researchers have found little relationship between gender and attitudes toward abortion (Cook, Jelen, and Wilcox, 1992).

14. Using a series of seven questions, NORC asks whether abortion should be allowed in the following situations: serious defect in the baby, the woman wants no more children, the woman's health is endangered, the family cannot afford any more children, the woman was raped, the woman is single, or the woman wants an abortion for any reason.

15. Between 1972 and 1994, NORC asked questions on abortion 128 times. For twenty-nine of these questions, there were statistically significant gender differences; on twenty-eight of these twenty-nine questions, men were more supportive of abortion rights than women.

16. Among women, those who were opposed to abortion were more likely than those who were pro-choice to have strong opinions about the issue. For example, women who opposed abortion in the case of a serious birth defect were more likely than those who were pro-choice to say they were very concerned about the abortion issue (64.8% v. 32.5%), that the issue was very important to them (45.7% v. 9.4%), and that their opinions were very unlikely to change (86.1% v. 59.0%).

17. Our findings are similar to those of Simon and Landis (1989). They examined a number of polls and found that since 1938 both men and women have been increasingly more supportive of women working outside the home and of women having equal opportunity with men in the workplace. With the exception that women were more likely than men to perceive sexual discrimination in the workplace, the authors found few notable differences between men and women.

18. The NORC questions discussed in this section were asked only in the years indicated.

19. Support by both men and women for guaranteeing these groups civil liberties increased for four of the five groups since the early 1970s. The increase was greatest in attitudes toward civil rights for homosexuals (63.2% in 1973 and 81.3% in 1994). There was no change in attitudes toward civil liberties for racists.

20. *Bureau of Justice Statistics*, edited by Maguire and Pastore (1993), reported that in 1992 the victimization rate for men over the age of twelve was 101.4 (per 100,000), while the victimization rate for women was 81.8. These data were derived from the Crime Victimization Survey.

21. The gap has declined somewhat in recent years (29.3% of men v. 13.1% of women in 1994; gap = 16.2) as women increasingly state that they have been threatened with a gun.

22. Amato and Booth (1995) found that over an eight-year period wives who adopted a less traditional gender role were more likely than other

women to perceive a drop in the quality of their marriage.

23. Respondents were asked to rank the job characteristics that were most important to them. Of the five categories, we have combined the first and second choice.

24. For a popular account of growing alienation among both Democrats and Republicans, see Harwood (1995).

25. The greater tendency of women to say that "sometimes politics and government seem so complicated that a person like me can't really understand what's going on" might be explained by the general tendency for men to express more confidence in their own intelligence. Researchers have found that men are more likely than women to overestimate their own IQ scores (Furnham and Rawles, 1995).

26. This tendency is not absolute, nor has it been observed in all years.

27. For example, in 1994, 43.6 percent of men said they rarely attended church, compared with 33.0 percent of women (gap = 10.6), and 43.2 percent of women and 33.5 percent of men (gap = 9.7) said they believed "that the Bible is God's word and all it says is true."

28. A detailed discussion of gender differences in voter participation is found in Chapter 3.

29. See England and McCreary (1987) for a discussion of the gender gap in income through 1983 and Goldin (1990) for an analysis of the gender gap in wages through 1987. Goldin found that the ratio of female to male earnings increased from .59 to .66 between 1971 and 1987 for median year-round earnings. A comparable change over the same time period occurred for median weekly wage and salary income (.68 to .70). Blau and Kahn (1994), using econometric modeling and data from Michigan Panel Study of Income Dynamics, also found substantial progress in women's relative wages between 1975 and 1987, even given the general increase in wage inequality in the United States. Cotter et al. (1995), using Census Public Use Microdata Samples (PUMS), found that between the 1980 and the 1990 census the ratio of female/male earnings increased 60 percent to 66 percent. They found that one-third of this increase was due to occupational desegregation and the remainder was due to declining earnings inequality within occupations.

30. Bernstein compares men and women within the same education and racial grouping, which controls for the effect of these variables, and also looks at hourly earnings, which controls for differences in hours worked per week.

31. Mishel and Bernstein (1994:124–125) believe that 71 percent of the reduction in the gender gap in wages between 1979 and 1989 can be explained by the falling wages of men.

32. By examining only those between the ages of twenty-five and forty-four, Bernstein controls for the fact that older people are generally less educated than younger people. In addition, by age twenty-five most people have finished their formal education.

33. The proportion of women who were employed and women who were homemakers does not add up to 100 percent because the following categories were not included: not employed, student, and retired. The percentage of men who were employed declined from 89.9 percent in 1952 to 73.4 percent in 1994 as men became more likely to say they were unemployed or retired.

34. Some analysts note that women disproportionately occupy the

lower rungs of professional occupations and that within many occupations there are still substantial segregation and income inequalities between men and women (Ferree, 1987; Reskin, 1991; and Almquist, 1991).

35. Our findings are not at odds with those who have also conducted large-scale studies of ideological differences between men and women in the general populace. These studies found that women were more liberal than men, especially in areas involving compassion and military intervention (Beutel and Marini, 1995; Baxter and Lansing, 1983; Shapiro and Mahajan, 1986; Deitch, 1988; Stoper, 1989; and Page and Shapiro, 1992). Studies of elites show that the ideological gaps between men and women are parallel but often larger than the gaps between men and women in the general population (Rapoport, Stone, and Abramowitz, 1990; Wilcox, Brown, and Powell, 1993).

36. The apparent inconsistencies concerning foreign policy and criminal justice issues may be more apparent than real. On one hand, women were more likely than men to be concerned about crime and to believe that the United States had a vital stake in foreign affairs. On the other hand, women were less likely than men to support punitive criminal sanctions or military intervention, advocating a more humanistic solution to some of these problems (increased spending for international drug prevention and combating world hunger, for example). With this interpretation, the positions of the Democratic Party on these two issues would probably induce women to vote Democratic.

3

The Gender Gap

A gender gap, or difference between the way women and men vote, existed long before the term began to be widely used. Since actual votes are not reported by sex, the only way to determine if there was a gender gap in an election is to look at survey data, which did not become commonly available until the early 1950s. Survey data from 1952 reveal a definite gender gap. There is even evidence that a gender gap may have existed ever since women began voting in 1920, although the data are scarce (Mueller, 1988).

The term "gender gap" was coined, and the phenomenon skillfully promoted, by feminists and women's organizations beginning in the early 1980s, after women started voting more Democratic than men (a reversal of the earlier gap, when women voted more Republican than men). Kathy Bonk (1988) has written an excellent account of how the National Organization for Women (NOW) and other women's organizations and leaders promoted awareness of the gender gap in order to draw attention to and increase the importance of women voters, to bolster the flagging campaign to pass the Equal Rights Amendment (ERA), and to pressure Walter Mondale into choosing a woman vice-presidential candidate.

By the 1980s it was becoming obvious that the ERA was in serious trouble and might die before the ratification deadline. According to Bonk, Ellie Smeal and other women leaders devised a campaign to highlight the gender gap and the importance of women voters, even issuing a monthly "Gender Gap Update" to several thousand reporters "in a simple, easy to read format" (Bonk, 1988: 92). Despite the fact that there was no evidence that the gender gap was related to views about the ERA, NOW and the ERA campaign promoted the gender gap in their efforts to pressure state legislators to vote for it.

When the ERA died in 1982, feminists claimed they would "remember each November" and emphasized Ronald Reagan's "problem with women." Both Ellie Smeal (1984) and Bella Abzug (1984) wrote books about the gender gap aimed at increasing the political influence of women. Smeal's was titled *Why and How Women Will Elect the Next President;* Abzug's was subtitled *A Guide to Political Power for American Women.* Despite the fact that there was no evidence that a woman vice-presidential candidate would attract additional women voters, women leaders effectively used the gender gap to convince Walter Mondale to choose a woman as his running mate (Frankovic, 1988).

In the end, women leaders and women's organizations succeeded in drawing a great deal of attention to the gender gap and in nominating the first major-party, woman vice-presidential candidate. At the same time, however, they lost the Equal Rights Amendment and watched as Ronald Reagan, who was a strong opponent of the issues they cared most about, beat Walter Mondale and Geraldine Ferraro by huge margins.

It is the *term* gender gap, rather then the gender gap itself, then, that began in the 1980s. The term has continued to be widely used ever since, but is poorly understood and frequently misused.

The gender gap is nothing more that the *difference* between the way men and women vote, and is quite different from "winning among women." A candidate can have more support from women than from men (a gender gap) and yet not win a majority of women's votes. For example, a candidate who received 40 percent of women's votes and 30 percent of men's votes would have a 10-point gender gap but would not have won among women.

And a candidate might have a large gender gap, win among women, and still lose the election. For example, a candidate who received 53 percent of women's votes and 33 percent of men's votes would have a 20-point gender gap and would have won a majority of women's votes, but not enough total votes to win the election.

Winning an election depends on the level of support a candidate receives, not on the gender gap. The gender gap does not and cannot ever elect anyone—it is simply the difference between the way women and men vote.

For consistency in this book, we calculate the gender gap in various races by subtracting the percentage of men who voted for the Democratic candidate from the percentage of women who voted for that candidate. This calculation will usually yield exactly the same number as subtracting the percentage of women who voted for the Republican candidate from the percentage of men who voted for that candidate.[1]

Whenever one candidate does better among women than among men, the other candidate has the same advantage among men. For example, a candidate who won 55 percent of women's votes and 50 percent of men's votes would have a 5-point gender gap or advantage among women voters. The candidate's opponent would have a 5-point advantage among men, having won 50 percent of men's votes and 45 percent of women's votes.

The term "gender gap" describes the difference between the way men and women vote, but it says nothing about what caused the difference. A gender gap is neutral; it is not necessarily good or bad for a candidate to have a gender gap. The gap could occur because women moved toward one candidate or because men moved toward the other, or some combination of the two. Individual candidates may find that their gender gaps vary from one election to the next as men and women move toward or away from that candidate or party.

Historical Changes in Voting

Tables 3.1 through 3.4 show data from a variety of survey organizations on gender gaps in presidential and congressional elections.[2] Figures 3.1 and 3.2 chart the gender gap using National Election Studies (NES) data. Although there are minor differences in any given year from one survey organization to another, the results are remarkably consistent overall.

Presidential Gender Gap

In presidential elections from 1952 to 1960, women were more likely than men to vote Republican.[3] The average gender gap (AG) for these three elections was 4.7, according to both NES data and Gallup.

With the exception of the 1976 election, since 1964 women have been more likely than men to vote for the Democratic presidential candidate.[4] This trend was particularly evident in the last four presidential elections. The average gender gaps since 1980 for the various polling organizations are shown below:[5]

NES	7.7
NORC	5.8
Gallup	6.0
LAT (*Los Angeles Times*)	6.5
NBC (1980–1988)[6]	8.0
CBS (1980–1988)	8.0
ABC (1980–1988)	7.3
VNS (Voter News Service, 1992)	4.0

Table 3.1 Presidential Voting and Gender Gap

		Democrat			Republican			Other		
	Year	Male	Female	Gap	Male	Female	Gap	Male	Female	Gap
NES										
Stevenson/Eisenhower	1952	43%	41%	–2	57%	59%	2	1%	0%	–1
Stevenson/Eisenhower	1956	43	37	–6	56	63	7	1	0	–1
Kennedy/Nixon	1960	52	46	–6	48	53	5	1	0	–1
Johnson/Goldwater	1964	65	69	4	34	31	–3	0	0	0
Humphrey/Nixon/Wallace	1968	38	43	5	47	48	1	15	9	–6
McGovern/Nixon	1972	32	38	6	67	61	–6	1	1	0
Carter/Ford	1976	50	51	1	48	48	0	3	1	–2
Carter/Reagan/Anderson	1980	36	42	6	55	48	–7	9	10	1
Mondale/Reagan	1984	37	45	8	62	54	–8	1	1	0
Dukakis/Bush	1988	43	50	7	56	50	–6	2	1	–1
Clinton/Bush/Perot	1992	42	52	10	35	33	–2	23	15	–8
NORC										
Humphrey/Nixon/Wallace	1968	41	45	4	46	50	4	13	5	–8
McGovern/Nixon	1972	39	41	2	59	58	–1	2	2	0
Carter/Ford	1976	56	54	–2	43	45	2	1	1	0
Carter/Reagan/Anderson	1980	43	49	6	50	45	–5	7	7	0
Mondale/Reagan	1984	37	41	4	63	59	–4	1	0	–1
Dukakis/Bush	1988	44	47	3	54	53	–1	2	0	–2
Clinton/Bush/Perot	1992	37	47	10	39	38	–1	24	15	–9
Gallup										
Stevenson/Eisenhower	1952	47	42	–5	53	58	5			
Stevenson/Eisenhower	1956	45	39	–6	55	61	6			
Kennedy/Nixon	1960	52	49	–3	48	51	3			
Johnson/Goldwater	1964	60	62	2	40	38	–2			
Humphrey/Nixon/Wallace	1968	41	45	4	43	43	0	16	12	–4
McGovern/Nixon	1972	37	38	1	63	62	–1			
Carter/Ford	1976	53	48	–5	45	51	6	1	0	–1

(continues)

Table 3.1 (continued)

	Year	Democrat			Republican			Other		
		Male	Female	Gap	Male	Female	Gap	Male	Female	Gap
Gallup (continued)										
Carter/Reagan/Anderson	1980	38%	44%	6	53%	49%	–4	7%	6%	–1
Mondale/Reagan	1984	36	45	9	64	55	–9			
Dukakis/Bush	1988	44	48	4	56	52	–4			
Clinton/Bush/Perot	1992	41	46	5	37	38	1	22	16	–6
LAT										
Carter/Reagan/Anderson	1980	35	41	6	51	44	–7	5	7	2
Mondale/Reagan	1984	36	43	7	63	56	–7			
Dukakis/Bush	1988	41	50	9	57	49	–8			
Clinton/Bush/Perot	1992	40	44	4	38	38	0	21	17	–4
NBC										
Carter/Reagan/Anderson	1980	36	45	9	56	47	–9	8	8	0
Mondale/Reagan	1984	36	45	9	64	55	–9			
Dukakis/Bush	1988	43	49	6	57	51	–6			
CBS/NYT (New York Times)										
Carter/Ford	1976	50	50	0	48	48	0			
Carter/Reagan/Anderson	1980	36	45	9	55	47	–8	7	7	0
Mondale/Reagan	1984	37	44	7	62	56	–6			
Dukakis/Bush	1988	41	49	8	57	50	–7			
ABC										
Carter/Reagan/Anderson	1980	35	42	7	54	47	–7	9	9	0
Mondale/Reagan	1984	38	46	8	62	54	–8			
Dukakis/Bush	1988	42	49	7	57	50	–7			
VNS										
Clinton/Bush/Perot	1992	41	45	4	38	38	0	21	17	–4

Note: NES, VNS, and NORC data combine "other" with major third-party candidates. CBS, ABC, NBC, and VNS exclude nonmajor third-party candidates. CBS, ABC, and NBC exit polls were not conducted in 1992, as they joined together into VNS/VRS.

Figure 3.1 Presidential Gender Gap, 1952–1992 (Percentage Democratic)

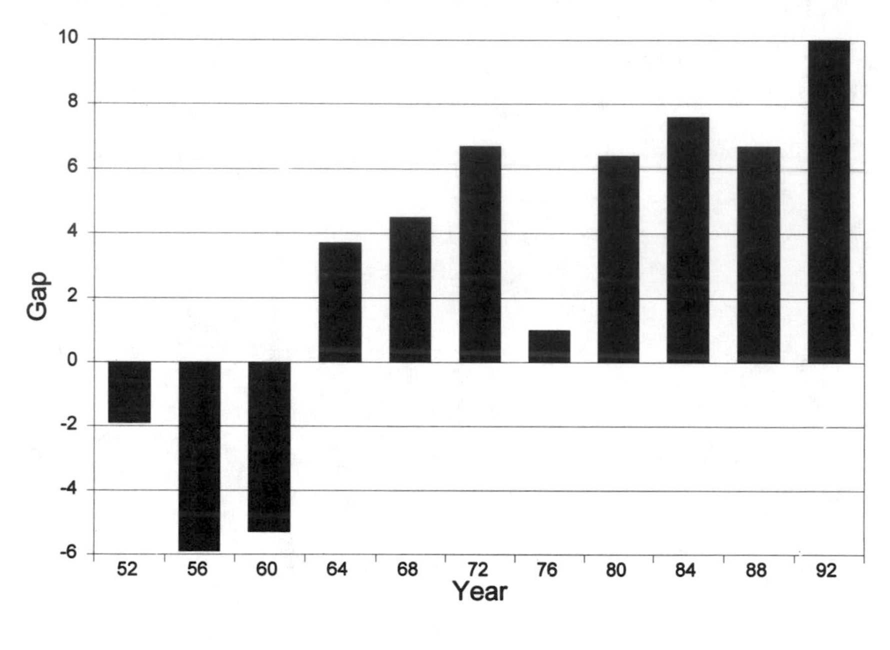

Source: NES

The gender gaps for each year and for each survey organization are shown in Table 3.2. There are three substantial differences among the results found by the various polling organizations:

1. NES data indicate a lower percentage of men relative to women voting for McGovern in 1972 (gap = 6). Gallup and National Opinion Research Center (NORC) show far smaller gaps (gaps = 2 and 1, respectively).
2. In 1976 Gallup data indicate that women were less likely than men to vote for Carter (gap = –5). NES and NORC show far smaller gaps (gaps = 1 and –2, respectively).
3. In 1992 NES and NORC (gap = 10 for both) show substantially larger gender gaps than Gallup (gap = 5), the *Los Angeles Times* (gap = 4), or VNS (gap = 4). This discrepancy clouds the debate about whether or not the gender gap is growing.

Table 3.2 Gender Gaps in Presidential Elections

Year	Party		NES	NORC	Gallup	LAT	NBC	CBS	ABC	VNS
1952	D	Stevenson	–2		–5					
	R	Eisenhower	2		5					
	I	Other	–1							
1956	D	Stevenson	–6		–6					
	R	Eisenhower	7		6					
	I	Other	–1							
1960	D	Kennedy	–6		–3					
	R	Nixon	5		3					
	I	Other	–1							
1964	D	Johnson	4		2					
	R	Goldwater	–3		–2					
	I	Other	0							
1968	D	Humphrey	5	4	4					
	R	Nixon	1	4	0					
	I	Wallace/Other	–6	–8	–4					
1972	D	McGovern	6	2	1					
	R	Nixon	6	–1	–1					
	I	Other	0	0						
1976	D	Carter	1	–2	–5			0		
	R	Ford	0	2	6			0		
	I	Other	–2	0	–1					
1980	D	Carter	6	6	6	6	9	9	7	
	R	Reagan	–7	–5	–4	–7	–9	–8	–7	
	I	Anderson/Other	1	0	–1	2	0	0	0	
1984	D	Mondale	8	4	9	7	9	7	8	
	R	Reagan	–8	–4	–9	–7	–9	–6	–8	
	I	Other	0	–1						
1988	D	Dukakis	7	3	4	9	6	8	7	
	R	Bush	–6	–1	–4	–8	–6	–7	–7	
	I	Other	–1	–2						
1992	D	Clinton	10	10	5	4				4
	R	Bush	–2	–1	1	0				0
	I	Perot/Other	–8	–9	–6	–4				–4

Codes: D- Democrat, R- Republican, I- Independent.

Congressional Gender Gap

Tables 3.3 and 3.4 and Figure 3.2 show similar data on congressional elections. Only NES has data available for elections before 1978, which is unfortunate since there are discrepancies among the survey organizations in recent years.[7] Nevertheless, the following conclusions can be drawn:

1. Between 1956 and 1966, women were more likely than men to vote Republican (AG = 4.2 using NES data).
2. Beginning in 1982[8] and continuing to the present, women have been more likely than men to vote for Democratic congressional candidates. The average gaps among the seven survey organizations ranged from 4.2 to 6.0.

Table 3.3 Congressional Vote: Percentage of Men and Women Who Voted Democratic

	Year	Male	Female	Gap
NES				
	1952	48	49	1
	1956	58	48	–10
	1958	61	60	–1
	1960	55	56	1
	1962	61	55	–6
	1964	65	65	0
	1966	62	53	–9
	1968	52	52	0
	1970	54	55	1
	1972	57	56	–1
	1974	63	61	–2
	1976	58	57	–1
	1978	60	58	–2
	1980	56	53	–3
	1982	54	60	6
	1984	53	57	4
	1986	59	62	3
	1988	59	59	0
	1990	59	69	10
	1992	57	62	5
	1994	45	49	4
Gallup				
	1970	53	55	2
	1978	53	57	4
	1982	53	58	5
	1984	48	53	5
	1992	51	58	7
	1994	43	49	6
LAT				
	1984	46	52	6
	1988	47	52	5
	1992	53	58	5
NBC				
	1982	52	58	6
	1986	53	56	3
CBS				
	1980	49	55	6
	1982	55	58	3
	1984	48	54	6
	1986	51	54	3
	1988	52	57	5
ABC				
	1982	56	61	5
	1984	47	53	6
	1986	53	58	5
	1988	49	56	7
VNS				
	1990	52	55	3
	1992	52	55	3
	1994	42	53	11

Note: Third-party candidates are excluded from the analysis of voting for congressional candidates. The Democratic vote and the Republican vote add up to 100%.

Table 3.4 Gender Gaps in Congressional Elections

Year	NES	Gallup	LAT	NBC	CBS	ABC	VNS
1952	1						
1956	–10						
1958	–1						
1960	1						
1962	–6						
1964	0						
1966	–9						
1968	0						
1970	1	2					
1972	–1						
1974	–2						
1976	–1						
1978	–2	4					
1980	–3				6		
1982	6	5		6	3	5	
1984	4	5	6		6	6	
1986	3			3	3	5	
1988	0		5		5	7	
1990	10						3
1992	5	7	5				3
1994	4	6					11

Although women have clearly been more likely than men to vote for Democratic congressional candidates since 1982, the differences in the gaps reported by each survey organization make it easy to misinterpret or overinterpret changes in the gender gap over time or in any given year.

Party Identification Gender Gap

Women and men are similarly different when it comes to expressing which political party they prefer. Tables 3.5 and 3.6 and Figure 3.3 display the gender gaps in men's and women's party preference.[9] The data indicate the following:

Except for 1944, women have consistently been less likely than men to classify themselves as independents. In other words, women have been more likely than men to express a preference for one of the two major political parties. For example, according to Gallup data from 1952, 44 percent of women and 41 percent of men said they were Democratic (gap = 3); 39 percent of women and 35 percent of men said they were Republican (gap = 4); and 17 percent of women and 24 percent of men said they were independent (gap = –7).

Between 1952 and 1964, women were more likely than men to identify with the Republican Party. The average gender gap for

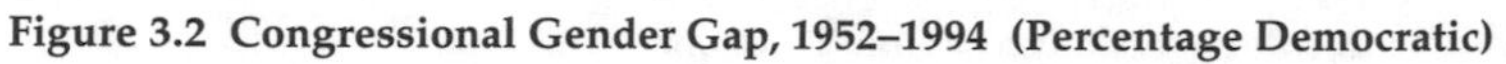

Figure 3.2 Congressional Gender Gap, 1952–1994 (Percentage Democratic)

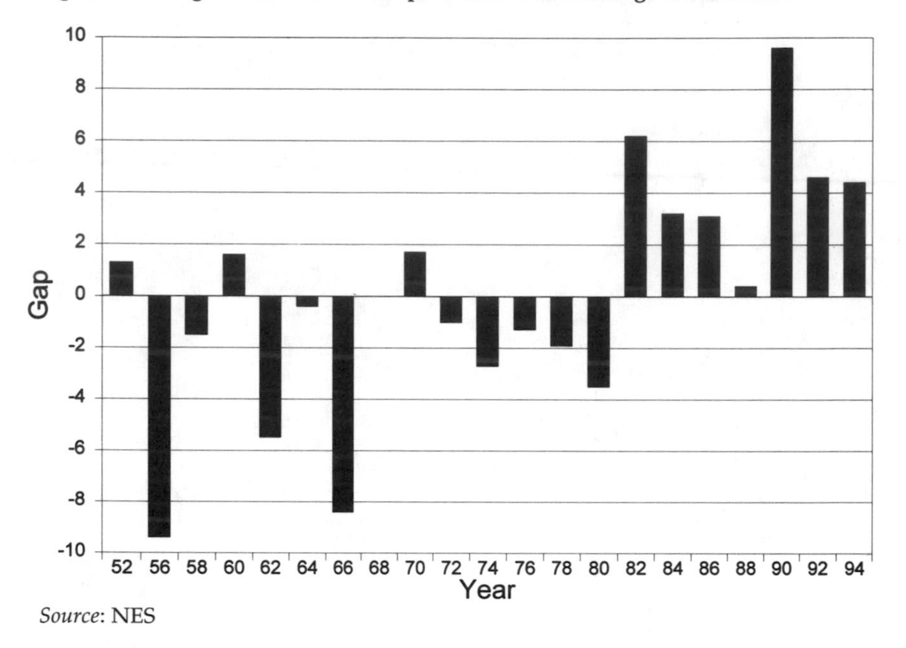

Source: NES

Figure 3.3 Party Identification Gender Gap, 1952–1994 (Percentage Democratic)

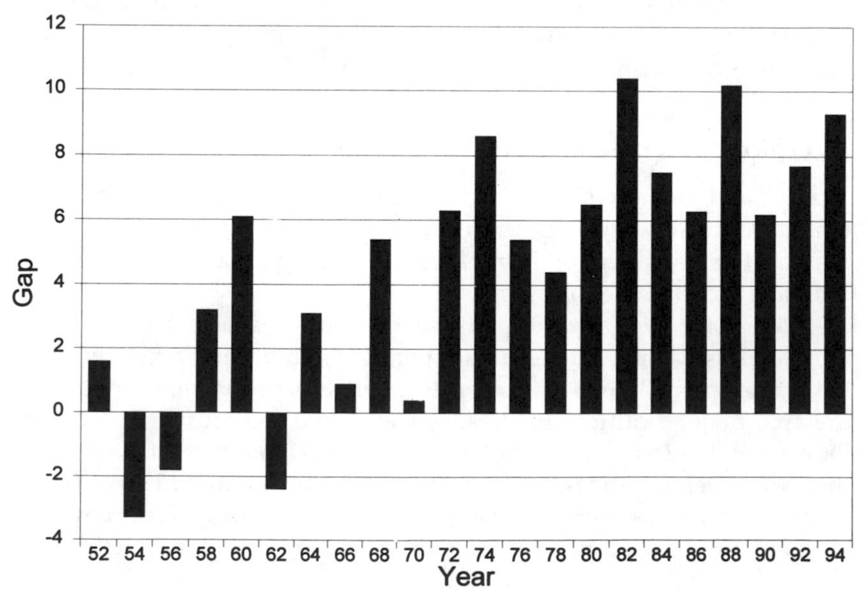

Source: NES

Table 3.5 Party Identification

Year	Democrat			Independent			Republican		
	Male %	Female %	Gap	Male %	Female %	Gap	Male %	Female %	Gap
NES									
1952	48	49	1	26	21	–5	26	30	4
1954	51	48	–3	24	22	–2	25	31	6
1956	46	45	–1	28	22	–6	26	34	8
1958	49	53	4	23	18	–5	28	30	2
1960	43	49	6	29	19	–10	28	32	4
1962	50	47	–3	24	20	–4	27	32	5
1964	51	54	3	26	21	–5	24	26	2
1966	46	47	1	30	28	–2	24	26	2
1968	43	48	5	32	28	–4	25	24	–1
1970	47	47	0	30	30	0	24	23	–1
1972	37	44	7	39	32	–7	23	24	1
1974	35	43	8	43	34	–9	23	23	0
1976	37	42	5	43	32	–11	21	26	5
1978	38	42	4	44	34	–10	19	23	4
1980	38	45	7	40	32	–8	22	24	2
1982	39	50	11	35	27	–8	26	23	–3
1984	34	41	7	39	32	–7	28	28	0
1986	37	44	7	38	30	–8	25	26	1
1988	30	40	10	42	32	–10	29	28	–1
1990	36	43	7	36	34	–2	27	23	–4
1992	32	40	8	40	37	–3	28	23	–5
1994	28	38	10	38	33	–5	33	29	–4
NORC									
1972	49	51	2	29	25	–4	22	24	2
1973	41	44	3	35	32	–3	24	24	0
1974	43	45	2	35	30	–5	22	25	3

(continues)

Table 3.5 (continued)

Year	Democrat			Independent			Republican		
	Male %	Female %	Gap	Male %	Female %	Gap	Male %	Female %	Gap
NES (continued)									
1975	40	42	2	41	34	–7	19	25	6
1976	38	46	8	41	34	–7	22	20	–2
1977	42	47	5	38	30	–8	21	23	2
1978	38	41	3	41	34	–7	21	25	4
1980	37	40	3	41	37	–4	22	24	2
1982	37	43	6	41	33	–8	22	23	1
1983	38	41	3	38	33	–5	24	26	2
1984	35	39	4	39	35	–4	26	26	0
1985	35	43	8	35	27	–8	29	31	2
1986	35	43	8	38	31	–7	27	26	–1
1987	37	42	5	35	31	–4	28	27	–1
1988	32	41	9	39	31	–8	30	28	–2
1989	32	41	9	32	27	–5	36	31	–5
1990	31	39	8	35	29	–6	34	32	–2
1991	30	41	11	36	30	–6	34	29	–5
1993	31	37	6	36	34	–2	33	29	–4
1994	34	39	5	37	32	–5	30	29	–1

Gallup

Year	Democrat			Independent			Republican			Other		
	Male %	Female %	Gap	Male %	Female %	Gap	Male %	Female %	Gap	Male %	Female %	Gap
1940	40	41	1	23	15	–8	34	38	4	3	5	2
1944	39	41	2	18	18	0	39	37	–2	1	1	0
1948	41	44	3	24	17	–7	35	39	4			
1952	41	44	3	24	17	–7	35	39	4			
1956	45	45	0	20	17	–3	34	38	4			
1960	50	50	0	25	23	–2	24	26	2			
1964	46	47	1	27	21	–6	27	31	4			

(continues)

Table 3.5 (continued)

Gallup (continued)

Year	Democrat			Independent			Republican			Other		
	Male %	Female %	Gap	Male %	Female %	Gap	Male %	Female %	Gap	Male %	Female %	Gap
1968	40	46	6	31	26	–5	29	28	–1			
1972	46	48	2	19	16	–3	35	36	1			
1976	39	43	4	38	30	–8	23	27	4			
1980	42	48	6	27	24	–3	31	28	–3			
1984	35	41	6	29	23	–5	36	36	0			
1988	33	42	9	28	25	–3	39	33	–6			
1992	34	41	7	30	25	–5	36	34	–2			

LAT Telephone[a]

Year	Democrat			Independent			Republican			Don't Know/ Other/Refused			Not Think In That Way[b]		
	Male %	Female %	Gap	Male %	Female %	Gap	Male %	Female %	Gap	Male %	Female %	Gap	Male %	Female %	Gap
1980	48	47	–1	20	20	0	23	23	0	9	10	1			
1982	47	50	3	18	18	0	30	27	–3	5	5	0			
1986	31	40	9	16	12	–4	33	28	–5	5	3	–2	15	17	2
1990	36	42	6	12	11	–1	36	28	–8	5	7	2	11	12	1
1994	33	44	11	15	15	0	36	29	–7	10	9	–1	6	3	–3

LAT Exit Polls

Year	Democrat			Independent			Republican			Other			Not Think In That Way[b]		
	Male %	Female %	Gap	Male %	Female %	Gap	Male %	Female %	Gap	Male %	Female %	Gap	Male %	Female %	Gap
1984	30	36	6	39	35	–4	31	29	–2						
1988	27	33	6	28	23	–5	33	28	–5	2	2	0	10	14	4
1992	37	45	8	25	19	–6	35	35	0	2	1	–1			

(continues)

Table 3.5 (continued)

CBS/NYT Exit Polls

Year	Democrat			Independent			Republican		
	Male %	Female %	Gap	Male %	Female %	Gap	Male %	Female %	Gap
1976	39	43	4	38	30	–8	23	27	4
1978	37	39	2	40	36	–4	23	25	2
1980	42	48	6	27	24	–3	31	28	–3
1982	43	48	5	26	22	–4	31	30	–1
1984	35	41	6	29	23	–6	36	35	–1
1988	33	42	9	28	25	–3	39	33	–6

ABC Exit Polls

Year	Democrat			Independent			Republican			Other		
	Male %	Female %	Gap	Male %	Female %	Gap	Male %	Female %	Gap	Male %	Female %	Gap
1980	37	43	6	31	25	–6	27	27	0	5	4	–1
1982	38	44	6	31	27	–4	27	26	–1	4	3	–1
1984	34	41	7	29	24	–5	33	32	–1	4	3	–1
1986	40	47	7	22	19	–3	36	33	–3	2	2	0
1988	37	46	9	21	16	–5	40	35	–5	2	2	0

VNS Exit Polls

Year	Democrat			Independent			Republican			Other		
	Male %	Female %	Gap	Male %	Female %	Gap	Male %	Female %	Gap	Male %	Female %	Gap
1990	33	39	6	30	27	–3	35	32	–3	2	1	–1
1992	34	41	7	26	22	–4	36	34	–2	4	4	0
1994	31	41	10	27	23	–4	38	33	–5	4	3	–1

a. The *Los Angeles Times* telephone survey data are not consistent in terms of proximity of date to the election. Respondents were interviewed after the elections in 1980, 1982, and 1990. The 1986 interviews occurred in July and the 1994 interviews occurred just before the elections. The exit polling occurred on the day of the elections.
b. This response indicated they did not think of themselves in terms of political party.

Table 3.6 Gender Gap in Party Identification

Year	Party	NES	NORC	Gallup	LAT	CBS	ABC	VNS
1940	D			1				
	I			–8				
	R			4				
	O			2				
1944	D			2				
	I			0				
	R			–2				
	O			0				
1948	D			3				
	I			–7				
	R			4				
1952	D	1		3				
	I	–5		–7				
	R	4		4				
1954	D	–3						
	I	–2						
	R	6						
1956	D	–1		0				
	I	–6		–3				
	R	8		4				
1958	D	–4						
	I	–5						
	R	2						
1960	D	6		0				
	I	–10		–2				
	R	4		2				
1962	D	–3						
	I	–4						
	R	5						
1964	D	3		1				
	I	–5		–6				
	R	2		4				
1966	D	1						
	I	–2						
	R	2						
1968	D	5		6				
	I	–4		–5				
	R	–1		–1				
1970	D	0						
	I	0						
	R	–1						
1972	D	7	2	2				
	I	–7	–4	–3				
	R	1	2	1				
1974	D	8	2					
	I	–9	–5					
	R	0	3					
1976	D	5	8	4		4		
	I	–11	–7	–8		–8		
	R	5	–2	4		4		
1978	D	4	3			2		
	I	–10	–7			–4		
	R	4	4			2		

(continues)

Table 3.6 (continued)

Year	Party	NES	NORC	Gallup	LAT	CBS	ABC	VNS
1980	D	7	3	6	–1	6	6	
	I	–8	–4	–3	0	–3	–6	
	R	2	2	–3	0	–3	0	
	O				1		–1	
1982	D	11	6		3	5	6	
	I	–8	–8		0	–4	–4	
	R	–3	–1		–3	–1	–1	
	O				0		–1	
1984	D	7	4	6	6	6	7	
	I	–7	–4	–6	–4	–6	–5	
	R	0	0	0	–2	–1	–1	
	O						–1	
1986	D	7	8		9		7	
	I	–8	–7		–4		–3	
	R	1	–1		–5		–3	
	O				–2		0	
	N				2			
1988	D	10	9	9	6	9	9	
	I	–10	–8	–3	–5	–3	–5	
	R	–1	–2	–6	–5	–6	–5	
	O				0		0	
	N				4			
1990	D	7	8		6			6
	I	–2	–6		–1			–3
	R	–4	–2		–8			–3
	O				2			–1
	N				1			
1992	D	8	6[a]	7	8			7
	I	–3	–2	–5	–6			–4
	R	–5	–4	–2	0			–2
	O				–1			0
1994	D	10	5		11			10
	I	–5	–5		0			–4
	R	–4	–1		–7			–5
	O				–1			–1
	N				–3			

a. NORC 1993 data used because no survey was conducted in 1992. Otherwise, this table ignores NORC results from odd years.

Codes: D-Democrat, I-Independent, R-Republican, O-Other, N-Not think of self in this way (LAT).

Republicans[10] during this time period was 3.5, using Gallup data, and 4.4, using NES. There was a smaller gender gap in Democratic identification.[11]

Since 1968 women have been more likely than men to identify with the Democratic Party. The gap in party identification has been growing and was in double digits in 1994 for three of the four survey organizations.

Not All Gaps Are Created Equal

Although the gender gap is significant and has a large impact on U.S. politics, the gender gap is not and never has been a chasm. To put the gender gap in perspective, one must look at voting differences among other demographic groups. For example, in the 1996 presidential election, the gap between black and white was 44 points,[12] the gap between rich and poor was 20 points, and the gap between young and old 10 points, whereas the gap between men and women was 4 points.

Tables 3.7 and 3.8 show the gaps for various demographic groups in the 1992 presidential election and in the 1990, 1992, and 1994 congressional elections.[13] Gender differences are displayed first so that the reader can easily compare the gender gap to other gaps.

In the congressional elections, only age and region gaps are somewhat smaller than the gender gap. These three elections years were not unusual. The comparative gaps were analyzed back to 1952 using NES data. In almost all years and for almost all variables, gender created a smaller gap than other divisions of U.S. society.

The more subgroups into which a population is divided, and the smaller the size of the subgroups, the more likely is it that the gap between subgroups will be larger. For example, the gap between the lowest-income fifth and the highest-income fifth was bigger than the gap between men and women in part because there are more categories. However, this does not take away from the fact that the differences between women and men are smaller than other differences. Women do not form a monolithic voting bloc the way that blacks do or, to a lesser extent, Jews, born-again Christians, and the poor.

Although it is true that there was a large gender gap in the 1992 elections,[14] other gaps have also grown. In general, the United States is becoming increasingly polarized in political affiliation and voting behavior.[15]

The Gender Gap Within Demographic Groupings

In this section we examine whether the gender gap exists uniformly across the entire population or whether it is concentrated in certain subgroups. In other words, is the gender gap found among blacks similar to that found among whites, is the gap among low-income people similar to that found among high-income people, is the gap found among well-educated people similar to that found among those who never finished high school?

Table 3.7 Gaps Compared: 1992 Presidential Election (VNS)

Demographic Group	Democrat	Republican	Perot
Gender			
Male	40.9%	37.9%	21.2%*
Female	45.3	37.5	17.3
Largest gap	4.4	0.4	3.9
Race			
White	39.0	40.5	20.5**
Black	83.1	10.2	6.7
Largest gap	44.1	30.3	13.8
Age			
18–29	43.5	34.3	22.2**
30–39	40.1	38.3	21.6
40–49	42.5	37.8	19.7
50–59	40.7	40.5	18.8
60+	49.6	37.9	12.5
Largest gap	9.5	6.2	9.7
Currently Married			
Yes	39.6	40.6	19.8**
Not mentioned[a]	51.1	30.4	18.5
Largest gap	11.5	10.2	1.3
Education			
Less HS	53.9	27.7	18.4**
HS grad	43.4	35.9	20.7
Some college	41.3	37.4	21.3
College grad	39.0	41.5	19.6
Postgraduate	50.2	35.9	14.0
Largest gap	14.9	13.8	7.3
Income			
Under $15,000	58.2	23.3	18.5**
$15,000–$30,000	44.6	35.2	20.2
$30,000–$50,000	40.6	38.4	21.0
Over $50,000	38.7	44.0	17.3
Largest gap	19.5	20.7	3.7
Region			
East	47.1	34.8	18.1**
Midwest	42.5	36.9	20.7
South	41.3	42.6	16.0
West	43.2	34.2	22.6
Largest gap	5.8	8.4	6.6
Population of area			
Over 500,000	58.3	28.5	13.2**
50,000–500,000	50.5	33.3	16.3
Suburban	40.7	38.7	20.6
10,000–50,000	38.8	41.7	19.5
Rural	39.5	40.1	20.5
Largest gap	19.5	13.2	7.4
Religion			
Protestant	36.4	45.3	18.2**
Catholic	44.3	35.3	20.4
Other Christian	39.1	38.4	22.5
Jewish	79.8	10.9	9.3
Other	52.5	26.3	21.1
None	61.8	17.8	20.4
Largest gap	43.4	34.4	13.2

(continues)

Table 3.7 (continued)

Demographic Group	Democrat	Republican	Perot
Born-again Christian			
Yes	30.5%	55.7%	13.8%**
Not Mentioned[a]	46.8	32.6	20.7
Largest gap	16.3	23.1	6.9
Party identification			
Democrat	77.3	9.6	13.1**
Republican	10.1	72.7	17.1
Independent	37.5	31.4	31.1
Largest gap	67.2	63.1	18.0
Political ideology			
Liberal	67.8	14.1	18.1**
Moderate	47.5	31.4	21.1
Conservative	18.3	64.0	17.7
Largest gap	49.5	49.9	3.4

* $p < .05$
** $p < .01$
a. VNS asked respondents if the category applied to them. Nonresponses are not the same as an answer of "no."

Table 3.8 Gaps Compared: 1990–1994 Congressional Elections (VNS)

Demographic Group	1990	1992	1994
Gender			
Male	52.1%**	52.2%**	41.6%**
Female	55.3	55.5	52.7
Largest gap	3.2	3.3	11.1
Race			
White	51.6**	49.9**	42.0**
Black	79.9	88.9	91.7
Largest gap	28.3	39.0	49.7
Age			
18–29	53.0	55.0**	49.4
30–39	54.1	52.9	46.3
40–49	54.3	52.6	47.3
50–59	52.0	52.1	44.7
60+	54.4	56.4	48.5
Largest gap	2.4	4.3	4.7
Currently married			
Yes	51.5**	50.3**	41.9**
Not mentioned[a]	60.1	60.7	54.4
Largest gap	8.6	10.4	12.5
Education			
Less HS	61.0**	67.5**	57.6**
HS grad	57.9	58.0	46.6
Some college	53.2	52.6	41.0
College grad	51.5	45.9	44.8
Postgraduate	53.8	54.8	56.8
Largest gap	9.5	21.6	16.6

(continues)

Table 3.8 (continued)

Demographic Group	1990	1992	1994
Income			
Under $15,000	64.6%**	68.8%**	61.8%**
$15,000–$30,000	56.5	57.1	51.3
$30,000–$50,000	53.9	52.2	45.1
Over $50,000	50.6	47.0	42.4
Largest gap	14.0	21.8	19.4
Region			
East	52.8**	55.5**	50.0*
Midwest	54.0	52.0	45.5
South	55.6	53.3	47.1
West	52.2	55.6	47.4
Largest gap	3.4	3.6	4.5
Population of area			
Over 500,000	60.9**	65.4**	72.2*
50,000–500,000	57.3	61.6	58.3
Suburban	53.1	51.2	42.7
10,000–50,000	30.9	50.7	44.1
Rural	52.5	50.5	43.3
Largest gap	30.0	14.9	29.5
Religion			
Protestant	47.5**	45.9**	39.3**
Catholic	57.2	56.8	47.1
Other Christian	57.1	50.7	47.8
Jewish	74.1	78.9	76.9
Other	68.8	66.2	65.1
None	60.2	69.6	62.6
Largest gap	26.6	33.0	37.6
Born-again Christian			
Yes	38.4**	40.6**	29.5**
Not mentioned[a]	54.6	57.1	50.5
Largest gap	16.2	16.5	21.0
Party identification			
Democrat	80.0**	88.8**	88.7**
Republican	25.8	15.2	8.3
Independent	53.5	54.8	41.5
Largest gap	54.2	73.6	80.4
Political ideology			
Liberal	73.7**	80.7**	81.4**
Moderate	57.8**	57.3	56.5
Conservative	38.8**	27.9	18.9
Largest gap	34.9	52.8	62.5

* $p < .05$
** $p < .01$
a. VNS asked respondents if the category applied to them. Nonresponses are not the same as an answer of "no."

In general, we find that the gender gap is uniform across most demographic categories; nevertheless, there are some interesting exceptions. In particular, consistently larger gender gaps are found among those who are employed, are in professional or managerial occupations, and have a college education.

Methodology

NES data go back to 1952 for both presidential and congressional elections. Unfortunately, the sample sizes for subgroups were often very small, especially in nonpresidential years. For example, NES interviewed just 51 blacks in 1952 and 189 blacks in 1992, making it very difficult to compare black males and black females. For that reason, in addition to using NES data, we used data from VNS exit polls between 1990 and 1994 that offered greater sample sizes. (For example, VNS interviewed 543 blacks in the 1992 presidential election.)

There are conceptual difficulties to consider in examining the gender gap among demographic subgroups. Whenever the subsample sizes are small, disparities must be very large to be statistically significant. Also, to determine the significance of a gender gap among any subgroup, one must consider the overall gender gap. For example, VNS data indicate an overall gender gap of 11.1 points in the 1994 congressional election, compared with an overall gap of 3.3 in 1992. A 10-point gender gap among a demographic subgroup in 1994 is therefore much less meaningful than a 10-point gap in 1992. Similarly, a small gender gap among a demographic subgroup would call for analysis in 1994, but it would not be as important in 1992.

The effects of twelve variables on the size of the gender gap were analyzed with VNS and NES data: race, age, marital status, employment status, education, income, region of country, community size, religion, religiosity, party identification, and ideological self-identification. In addition, NES data were used to analyze occupation.

To determine the significance of the gender gap for each demographic subgroup, we subtracted the gender gap within each demographic subgroup from the overall gender gap for that year. For example, in 1994 the gender gap among black respondents was 7.3. Subtracted from the 11.1 overall gender gap, we obtained a gap difference (GD) of 3.8 and concluded that there was a gender gap among black respondents, but it was smaller than the gap found among most other respondents.

To distinguish between large and small gaps, we used a 5-point decision rule. If the gender gap among the demographic subgroup was 5 points greater than or less than the overall gender gap, it was considered substantively interesting. Furthermore, the difference had to be statistically significant.[16] For example, in 1994 a gender gap of less than 6.1 points (11.1 – 5.0) within a particular demographic subgroup would be considered unusually small. This methodology allowed us to pay special attention to gaps that were either unusually larger or unusually smaller than average.

The results from the VNS data analysis are displayed in Tables 3.9 and 3.10. Because of the far smaller sample sizes, we used the NES data more for broad trends than to analyze gender gaps in individual years.[17]

Findings

In the election cycles of 1990, 1992, and 1994, the gender gap was fairly consistent across most demographic categories: race, age,[18] income,[19] region of country,[20] population density, religion, religiosity, party identification, and self-identified political ideology.[21] In other words, the gender gap was similar for blacks and whites, for old and young, rich and poor, and so on. However, there were some interesting exceptions, which are discussed below.

Employment Status. In the 1992[22] congressional and presidential elections, women who were employed full-time were much more likely to vote Democratic (gap = 11.7, GD = 8.4; gap = 8.6, GD = 4.2; respectively). Furthermore, employed women were particularly likely to vote for the Democratic presidential candidates from 1952 to 1972 (average GD = 6.1) and for Democratic congressional candidates prior to 1960 (average GD = 6.5).

However, one cannot assume that employed women were always more likely than women who were homemakers to vote Democratic. Figure 3.4 displays the gap in congressional elections between employed women and women who were homemakers from 1952 to 1994.[23] Women who were employed were more likely than homemakers to vote Democratic in 1952–1958, 1970–1974, and 1984–1986. However, homemakers were significantly more likely than employed women to vote Democratic in 1982 (68.5% of homemakers v. 57.6% of employed women; gap = 10.9) and, to a lesser extent, in 1980.

Occupation. NES data indicate that since 1952 the gender gap has been higher for professional and managerial employees (AG = 6.9, GD = 6.8 in congressional elections; and AG = 9.8, GD = 7.3 in presidential elections) than for the population at large.[24] Although this difference did not occur in every year, it occurred through all four decades of the study.

Little difference was found between clerical and sales workers and the population in general. However, since 1952 the gender gap in presidential elections has been greater for blue-collar workers than for the population at large (AG = 10.6; GD = 8.2).

Table 3.9 Gender Gap, by Demographic Subgroup, 1992 Presidential Election (VNS Data)

Demographic Group	Democrat	Republican	Perot
Overall			
Male	40.9%	37.9%	21.2%
Female	45.3	37.5	17.3
Gap	4.4	–0.4	–3.9
Race			
White			
Male	37.3	40.3	22.5**
Female	40.5	40.8	18.7
Gap	3.2	0.5	–3.8
Black			
Male	77.9	13.5	8.6**
Female	86.9	7.7	5.4
Gap	9.0	–5.8	–3.2
Age			
18–29			
Male	38.2	36.5	25.4**
Female	47.9	32.5	19.6
Gap	9.7	–4.0	–5.8
30–39			
Male	37.4	39.0	23.6**
Female	42.0	38.0	20.0
Gap	4.6	–1.0	3.6
40–49			
Male	40.3	38.1	21.6**
Female	44.6	37.9	17.5
Gap	4.3	–0.2	–4.1
50–59			
Male	39.8	40.9	19.4
Female	41.6	40.3	18.1
Gap	1.8	–0.6	–1.3
60+			
Male	49.1	36.2	14.8**
Female	50.1	40.0	10.0
Gap	1.0	3.8	–4.8
Marital Status			
Married			
Male	37.6	41.8	20.6
Female	40.6	40.2	19.2
Gap	3.0	–1.6	–1.4
Never Married			
Male	45.8	32.2	21.9**
Female	55.4	29.3	15.3
Gap	9.6	–2.9	–6.6
Widowed			
Male	63.2	22.8	14.1
Female	54.6	35.7	9.7
Gap	–8.6	12.9	–4.4
Div/Sep			
Male	50.5	23.2	26.3*
Female	48.8	32.0	19.2
Gap	–1.7	8.8	–7.1

(continues)

Table 3.9 (continued)

Demographic Group	Democrat	Republican	Perot
Employment Status			
Employed full			
Male	36.8%	41.1%	22.1%**
Female	45.4	35.2	19.5
Gap	8.6	–5.9	–2.6
Employed part			
Male	48.1	28.7	23.2
Female	45.1	36.3	18.7
Gap	–3.0	7.6	–4.5
Student			
Male	44.8	34.0	21.2*
Female	52.6	37.3	10.1
Gap	7.8	3.3	–11.1
Out of work			
Male	53.1	25.6	21.4
Female	53.1	28.1	18.8
Gap	0.0	2.5	–2.6
Retired			
Male	48.5	34.4	17.0**
Female	49.7	40.1	10.1
Gap	1.2	5.7	–6.9
Homemaker v. employed (women only)			
Employed	45.4	35.2	19.5
Homemaker	36.0	45.0	19.0
Gap	–9.4	9.8	–0.5
Education			
Less HS			
Male	47.8	30.2	21.9
Female	57.4	26.9	15.7
Gap	9.6	–3.3	–6.2
HS grad			
Male	43.4	32.9	23.6**
Female	43.3	38.3	18.4
Gap	–0.1	5.4	–5.2
Some college			
Male	40.1	36.6	23.3*
Female	42.0	39.0	19.1
Gap	1.9	2.4	–4.2
College grad			
Male	34.0	43.0	23.0**
Female	43.6	39.9	16.5
Gap	9.6	–3.1	–6.5
Postgrad			
Male	47.3	40.1	12.7**
Female	54.7	30.4	14.9
Gap	7.4	–9.7	2.2
Income			
Under $15,000			
Male	57.7	20.6	21.6**
Female	58.3	25.2	16.5
Gap	0.6	4.6	–5.1

(continues)

Table 3.9 (continued)

Demographic Group	Democrat	Republican	Perot
Income (continued)			
$15,000–$30,000			
Male	42.1%	35.0%	22.8%**
Female	46.4	35.7	18.0
Gap	4.3	0.7	–4.8
$30,000–$50,000			
Male	37.7	39.6	22.7**
Female	43.1	37.4	19.5
Gap	5.4	–2.2	–3.2
$50,000+			
Male	37.1	44.5	18.4
Female	40.1	43.6	16.3
Gap	3.0	–0.9	–2.1
Region			
East			
Male	43.4	35.0	21.6**
Female	50.3	34.6	15.1
Gap	6.9	–0.4	–6.5
Midwest			
Male	40.6	37.1	22.3
Female	43.5	37.0	19.5
Gap	2.9	–0.1	1.5
South			
Male	39.0	43.0	18.0**
Female	43.0	42.7	14.3
Gap	4.0	–0.3	–3.7
West			
Male	41.5	34.7	23.7
Female	45.1	33.9	21.0
Gap	3.6	–0.8	–2.7
Population of Area			
Over 500,000			
Male	54.2	29.6	16.2**
Female	61.6	28.3	10.0
Gap	7.4	–1.3	–6.2
50,000–500,000			
Male	47.1	34.2	18.6**
Female	53.4	32.1	14.4
Gap	6.3	–2.1	–4.2
Suburbs			
Male	39.0	39.5	21.5*
Female	42.1	38.3	19.6
Gap	3.1	–1.2	–1.9
10,000–50,000			
Male	34.6	42.3	23.1**
Female	41.7	41.7	16.6
Gap	5.8	–0.6	–6.5
Rural			
Male	37.9	38.9	23.3**
Female	40.3	41.4	18.2
Gap	2.4	2.5	–5.1

(continues)

Table 3.9 (continued)

Demographic Group	Democrat	Republican	Perot
Religion			
Protestant			
Male	34.0%	46.6%	19.5%*
Female	38.5	44.3	17.1
Gap	4.5	–2.3	–2.4
Catholic			
Male	39.6	38.1	22.2**
Female	46.4	34.5	19.1
Gap	6.8	–3.6	–2.9
Other Christian			
Male	37.9	35.3	26.8*
Female	39.8	40.2	20.0
Gap	1.9	4.9	–6.8
Jewish			
Male	76.7	14.8	8.6
Female	86.3	7.7	5.9
Gap	9.6	–7.7	–2.7
Other			
Male	49.0	27.9	23.2
Female	55.5	24.8	19.7
Gap	6.5	–3.1	–3.5
None			
Male	56.8	20.3	22.8*
Female	68.0	15.4	16.6
Gap	11.2	–4.9	–6.2
Born-again Christian			
Yes			
Male	30.6	54.3	15.1
Female	30.4	56.4	13.3
Gap	–0.2	2.1	–1.8
Not mentioned[a]			
Male	43.6	33.8	22.6**
Female	49.3	32.0	18.7
Gap	5.7	–1.8	–3.9
Attend weekly religious services			
Yes			
Male	37.9	40.3	21.8
Female	41.0	36.7	22.3
Gap	3.1	–3.6	0.5
Not mentioned[a]			
Male	42.9	36.2	21.0**
Female	48.0	37.2	14.8
Gap	5.1	1.0	–6.2
Party Identification			
Democrat			
Male	76.4	8.8	14.7**
Female	77.8	10.2	12.0
Gap	1.4	1.4	–2.7
Republican			
Male	10.6	70.8	18.6*
Female	9.8	74.5	15.8
Gap	–0.8	3.7	–2.8

(continues)

Table 3.9 (continued)

Demographic Group	Democrat	Republican	Perot
Party Identification (continued)			
Independent			
Male	35.1%	32.2%	32.7%**
Female	40.2	30.5	29.3
Gap	5.1	–1.7	–3.4
Ideology			
Liberal			
Male	65.2	15.0	19.8
Female	69.1	14.1	16.8
Gap	3.9	–0.9	–3.0
Moderate			
Male	47.4	29.3	23.3**
Female	47.4	33.2	19.5
Gap	0.0	3.9	–3.8
Conservative			
Male	16.1	64.6	19.3*
Female	19.4	64.6	16.0
Gap	3.3	0.0	–3.2

* $p < .05$
** $p < .01$
a. VNS asked respondents if the category applied to them. It is not safe to assume that nonresponses indicate a "no" answer to the question.

Education. Among those who did not attend college, the gender gap in congressional voting in 1992 and especially in 1994 was markedly different from the general populace, according to VNS data. For example, in 1994 men without high school degrees were more likely than women without high school degrees (58.6% v. 55.4%; gap = 3.2; GD = 14.3), and more likely than men in the general population (41.6%), to vote Democratic. The opposite of this was true for those who graduated from college or had postgraduate education. The gender gap from 1990 to 1994 in congressional elections was greater for college graduates than for the general population (among college graduates average GD = 3.5; among those with postgraduate education average GD = 7.1).

The relationship between education and the gender gap was different for the 1992 presidential election. In this case, women with less than a high school degree were more apt than men to vote for Bill Clinton (gap = 9.6; GD = 5.2). In addition, women who had postgraduate education were particularly likely to vote for Ross Perot (14.9% of women and 12.7% of men voting for Perot; gap = 2.2; GD = 6.1) and less likely to vote for George Bush (gap = 9.7; GD = 9.3).

NES data also indicate that since 1984, men with less than a high

Table 3.10 Gender Gap, by Demographic Subgroup: Percentage Voting Democratic, 1990–1994 Congressional Elections (VNS)

Demographic Group	1990	1992	1994
Overall			
Male	52.1%**	52.2%**	41.6%**
Female	55.3	55.5	52.7
Gap	3.2	3.3	11.1
Race			
White			
Male	49.8**	48.8*	36.7**
Female	53.1	50.9	47.0
Gap	3.3	2.1	10.3
Black			
Male	79.8	84.5**	87.5**
Female	80.6	92.1	94.8
Gap	0.8	7.6	7.3
Age			
18–29			
Male	49.9**	52.1**	42.2**
Female	56.2	58.0	56.7
Gap	6.3	5.9	14.5
30–39			
Male	52.7	51.0*	40.7**
Female	55.2	54.5	51.3
Gap	2.5	3.5	10.9
40–49			
Male	53.1	51.0	40.4**
Female	55.4	53.9	53.7
Gap	2.3	2.9	10.6
50–59			
Male	49.4*	49.5	40.8**
Female	53.9	54.1	48.7
Gap	4.5	4.6	7.9
60+			
Male	53.6	56.2	43.2**
Female	55.1	56.7	53.2
Gap	1.5	0.5	10.0
Marital Status (Yes, No)[a,b]			
Married			
Male	50.2*	48.2*	36.8**
Female	52.7	51.4	47.0
Gap	2.5	3.2	10.2
Not mentioned			
Male	58.1*	57.7**	48.1**
Female	62.1	63.3	60.0
Gap	4.0	5.6	11.9
Marital Status			
Married			
Male		48.2*	
Female		51.4	
Gap		3.2	
Never married			
Male		55.0**	
Female		66.8	
Gap		11.8	

(continues)

Table 3.10 (continued)

Demographic Group	1990	1992	1994
Marital Status (continues)			
Widowed			
Male		67.1	
Female		56.1	
Gap		–11.0	
Div/Sep			
Male		62.7	
Female		62.9	
Gap		0.2	
Employment Status			
Employed full[c]			
Male	54.0**	47.0**	
Female	60.9	58.7	
Gap	6.9	11.7	
Employed part			
Male		61.8	
Female		56.2	
Gap		–5.6	
Student			
Male	49.7	56.1	
Female	56.4	54.4	
Gap	6.7	–1.7	
Out of work			
Male	49.3	65.3	
Female	49.6	62.8	
Gap	0.3	–2.5	
Retired			
Male	56.0	56.5	
Female	54.8	56.0	
Gap	–1.2	–0.5	
Homemaker v. employed (women only)			
Employed	60.9**	58.7**	
Homemaker	47.0	48.2	
Gap	–13.9	–10.5	
Education			
Less HS			
Male	61.1	67.1	58.6
Female	61.9	65.2	55.4
Gap	0.8	–1.9	–3.2
HS grad			
Male	57.6	59.0	43.5
Female	57.9	57.0	49.3
Gap	0.3	–2.0	5.8
Some college			
Male	51.8	50.6	34.1**
Female	54.3	54.6	47.1
Gap	2.5	4.0	13.0
College grad			
Male	48.4**	43.0*	36.5**
Female	55.0	48.5	52.6
Gap	6.6	5.5	16.1

(continues)

Table 3.10 (continued)

Demographic Group	1990	1992	1994
Education (continued)			
Postgrad			
Male	49.5%**	49.4%**	49.0%**
Female	59.1	61.9	65.8
Gap	9.6	12.5	16.8
Income			
Under $15,000			
Male	66.9	69.6	55.8**
Female	64.0	68.4	66.6
Gap	–2.9	–1.6	10.8
$15,000–$30,000			
Male	56.3	55.3	47.2**
Female	56.5	58.7	54.1
Gap	0.2	3.4	6.9
$30,000–$50,000			
Male	51.4**	49.5**	39.7**
Female	56.4	54.7	50.4
Gap	5.0	5.2	10.7
$50,000+			
Male	48.0**	45.8	36.3**
Female	53.8	47.7	49.5
Gap	5.8	1.9	13.2
Region			
East			
Male	50.6**	53.7*	44.1**
Female	55.0	57.6	55.6
Gap	4.4	3.9	11.5
Midwest			
Male	53.3	51.2	39.9**
Female	54.6	52.5	51.1
Gap	1.3	1.3	11.2
South			
Male	53.5**	51.1*	40.9**
Female	57.4	54.9	52.3
Gap	3.9	3.8	11.4
West			
Male	50.2*	53.2*	42.0**
Female	53.6	57.7	52.4
Gap	3.4	4.5	10.4
Population of Area			
Over 500,000			
Male	56.5**	63.6	68.6
Female	64.7	66.4	74.8
Gap	8.2	2.8	6.2
50,000–500,000			
Male	55.1*	59.7	50.3**
Female	59.4	63.4	66.6
Gap	4.3	3.7	16.3
Suburbs			
Male	51.9*	48.2**	37.8**
Female	54.2	53.6	47.1
Gap	2.3	5.4	9.3

(continues)

Table 3.10 (continued)

Demographic Group	1990	1992	1994
Population of Area (continued)			
10,000–50,000			
Male	30.7%	48.8%	38.1%**
Female	31.5	52.5	50.6
Gap	0.8	3.7	12.5
Rural			
Male	51.4	51.0	36.7**
Female	53.0	50.2	48.9
Gap	1.6	–0.8	12.2
Religion			
Protestant			
Male	45.2**	44.4	34.8**
Female	49.4	47.1	43.1
Gap	4.2	2.7	8.3
Catholic			
Male	54.7**	52.0**	39.3**
Female	59.5	59.9	54.9
Gap	4.8	7.9	15.6
Other Christian			
Male	58.7	49.2	39.3**
Female	55.6	52.7	54.5
Gap	–3.1	3.5	15.2
Jewish			
Male	71.9	75.9	80.0
Female	76.8	80.5	73.9
Gap	4.9	4.6	–6.1
Other			
Male	66.9	60.0*	58.8
Female	70.1	69.3	70.4
Gap	3.2	9.3	11.6
None			
Male	56.5*	63.3**	52.7**
Female	65.0	79.1	78.0
Gap	8.5	15.8	25.3
Born-again Christian			
Yes			
Male	38.7	40.8	23.3**
Female	39.0	41.4	34.7
Gap	0.3	0.6	11.4
Not mentioned[a]			
Male	52.7**	54.2**	44.6**
Female	56.1	59.3	55.9
Gap	3.4	5.1	11.3
Attend weekly religious services			
Yes			
Male		47.2**	
Female		52.8	
Gap		5.6	
Not mentioned[a]			
Male		53.9*	
Female		57.4	
Gap		3.5	

(continues)

Table 3.10 (continued)

Demographic Group	1990	1992	1994
Party ID			
Democrat			
Male	79.8%	89.0%	86.0%**
Female	79.9	88.6	90.4
Gap	0.1	–0.4	4.4
Republican			
Male	25.6	15.9	8.3
Female	26.0	14.9	8.4
Gap	0.4	–1.0	0.1
Independent			
Male	52.1	52.6**	36.0**
Female	54.8	57.7	47.7
Gap	2.7	5.1	11.7
Ideology			
Liberal			
Male	73.3	81.1	72.8**
Female	73.8	80.2	87.5
Gap	0.5	–0.9	14.7
Moderate			
Male	57.9	56.2	54.7
Female	57.5	57.9	57.8
Gap	–0.4	1.7	3.1
Conservative			
Male	36.2**	25.6*	15.8**
Female	41.9	30.2	22.9
Gap	5.7	4.6	7.1

* $p < .05$
** $p < .01$

a. VNS asked respondents if the category applied to them. It is not safe to assume that non-responses indicate "no" to the question.

b. In 1990 and 1994, VNS asked respondents if being married applied to them. In 1992 respondents were asked a full marital status question. The data are reported both ways.

c. In 1990 VNS did not ask respondents if they were employed. Instead, respondents were asked a combined occupation/employment question. This shows respondents who said they were professional, managerial, teachers, other white-collar, blue-collar, and farm.

school degree were somewhat more likely than other men to vote for Democratic congressional candidates, thus generating a smaller than expected or even negative gender gap (average GD = 7.6). A similar tendency occurred in the presidential elections in 1984 (gap = 2.6; GD = 10.2) and 1992 (gap = 1.2; GD = 7.5). Similar to the findings using VNS data, NES data found that women who graduated from college were appreciably more likely than men who were college graduates to vote Democratic in congressional elections since 1952 (average GD = 6.9) and in presidential elections between 1952 and 1960 (average GD = 13.6) and between 1984 and 1992 (average GD = 7.4).

Figure 3.4 Employed Versus Homemaker Gap, 1952–1994 (Percentage Democratic)

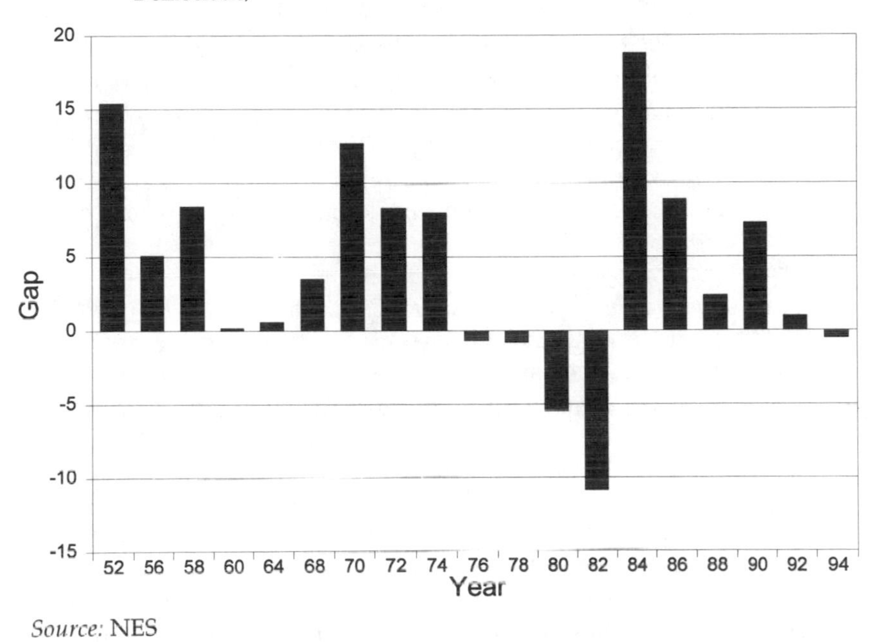

Source: NES

Marital Status. Women who had never married were more likely than men who had never married to vote for the Democratic candidates in the 1992 presidential (gap = 9.6; GD = 5.2) and congressional (Gap = 11.8; GD = 8.5) elections.[25] Furthermore, in those elections, female respondents who were widowed were less likely than male respondents who were widowed to vote for Bill Clinton (54.6% v. 63.2%; gap = 8.6; GD = 13.0) and the Democratic congressional candidates (56.1% v. 67.1%; gap = 11.0; GD = 14.3).

NES data indicate that marital status had little impact on the gender gap in recent years. However, between 1956 and 1964 men who had never married were much more likely than women who had never married to vote Democratic in congressional elections (AG = 29.1; average GD = 26.1) and in the 1960 presidential election (gap = 38.9; GD = 33.5).

Conclusions

Although generally consistent for most demographic groups, the size of the gender gap was somewhat influenced by factors often associated with class.[26] Recent gender gaps were greatest among those who were employed, in professional and managerial positions, and who had college education. In Chapter 6 we will see that these factors are not sufficient by themselves to explain the gender gap. One must go beyond demographic characteristics and also examine the relationship between political and social attitudes and the gender gap.

Women as Voters

Introduction

Women in the United States have had the right to vote since 1920. The passage of the Nineteenth Amendment culminated a seventy-year struggle to which thousands of women devoted their lives, and it was accompanied by a great deal of anxiety and fear on the part of men. One senator claimed it would "convert all the new harmonious elements of society into a state of war, and make every home a hell on earth" (Flexner 1975:151). A reporter wrote that war between the sexes had all but been declared (Mueller, 1988:19). Suffrage was finally approved when a twenty-four-year-old state legislator in Tennessee changed his mind about the amendment after receiving a telegram from his mother that said "Hurrah, and vote for suffrage!" (Flexner, 1975:336).

There was widespread expectation that an organized women's party, or at least a powerful women's voting bloc, would develop. Yet this never happened, and women didn't take advantage of the hard-fought right to vote at the same rate as men until the 1970s.[27]

By 1964—the first time the U.S. Census Bureau asked people whether they had voted—women made up a majority of reported voters, and they have continued to do so ever since. The impact of women as voters can be quantified both as a percentage of voters and by turnout rates, which measure the percentage of people eligible to vote who actually go to the polls. Women have been the majority of voters since 1964 because there have been more voting-age women than men in the population, even though their turnout rate was lower than men's until the mid-1970s.

Because election results are not reported by sex, the two methods commonly used to determine voter turnout rate by sex are exit polls and polls that ask men and women after the fact whether they voted. Weaknesses exist with both methods. When respondents are asked whether or not they voted, 5 percent to 15 percent say they voted when they did not (see Table 3.13). In essence, people like to give the socially correct response. Because of this problem with the data, it is theoretically possible that supposed turnout differences between men and women could be entirely due to different levels of misreporting.

Exit polls have been done by newspapers, wire services, and television networks since the late 1970s. The sampling is by polling place rather than by individual. Because interviewing is done right outside the polls, misreporting is not an issue. (The problems related to exit polls are discussed in Appendix 1.)

Voter Turnout Among Men and Women[28]

Estimates by the U.S. Census Bureau and NES of the gender gap in voter turnout differ (see Tables 3.11 and 3.12).[29] NES data going back to 1952 show gaps of more than 10 points before 1960, with women saying they voted less often than men. Between 1964 (the first year Census asked questions on voting behavior) and 1970, both surveys show women saying they voted about 5 points less than men.[30] After 1970 Census data show the gap narrowing and, beginning in 1984, a tendency for women to vote at a higher rate than men.[31] However, NES data indicate that women still vote at a lower rate than men.

There are two possible explanations for the discrepancy between Census and NES estimates on voting behavior:

Table 3.11 Reported Voting, Bureau of the Census

	Males Percent Voting	Females Percent Voting	Vote Gap	Voters Who Were Female
1964	71.9%	67.0%	–4.9	51.1%
1966	58.2	53.0	–5.2	50.9
1968	69.8	66.0	–3.8	51.9
1970	56.8	52.7	–4.1	51.4
1972	64.1	62.0	–2.1	52.3
1974	46.2	43.4	–2.8	51.4
1976	59.6	58.8	–0.8	52.6
1978	46.6	45.3	–1.3	52.2
1980	59.1	59.4	0.3	53.0
1982	48.7	48.4	–0.4	52.7
1984	59.0	60.8	1.9	53.5
1986	45.8	46.1	0.3	52.8
1988	56.4	58.3	1.8	53.3
1990	44.6	45.4	0.7	52.8
1992	60.2	62.3	2.1	53.2
1994	44.4	44.9	0.6	52.5

Table 3.12 Reported Voting, NES

	Male	Female	Gap	*p*
1952	79.7%	69.3%	–10.4	0.0001
1956	79.5	67.6	–11.9	0.0001
1958	66.7	49.6	–17.1	0.0001
1960	84.1	74.7	–9.4	0.0001
1962	63.7	57.7	–6.0	0.03
1964	80.2	75.6	–4.6	0.04
1966	65.2	59.9	–5.3	0.05
1968	78.1	74.1	–4.0	0.08
1970	61.9	57.5	–4.4	0.09
1972	76.4	70.1	–6.3	0.001
1974	56.2	49.9	–6.3	0.002
1976	76.9	67.8	–9.1	0.0001
1978	55.3	53.9	–1.4	0.5
1980	73.3	69.8	–3.5	0.1
1982	63.1	58.1	–5.0	0.06
1984	73.6	73.6	0.0	0.9
1986	52.8	52.3	–0.5	0.8
1988	72.2	67.8	–4.4	0.05
1990	48.8	44.8	–4.0	0.08
1992	76.6	73.9	–2.7	0.1
1994	60.4	56.7	–3.7	0.3

1. NES has a far higher nonresponse rate than the Census (25% v. 5%). Given that polling organizations have higher nonresponse rates among men than among women and that people who cannot be interviewed may be less likely to vote, it is possible that NES is less likely than the Census to interview men who don't vote.[32]

2. For all years, a lower percentage of respondents claim to have voted when interviewed by the Bureau of the Census than by NES. Among men, the average difference in reported voting rates between Census and NES was 11.2 since 1964. The corresponding difference among women was lower (8.3).[33] Men may be more likely to misreport their voting behavior when asked by NES than when they are asked by the Bureau of the Census.

One further point on the problem of measuring voting requires elaboration. Men may be more likely than women to misreport their vote.[34] NES periodically visits or calls voter registration offices to investigate whether people who claim to have voted actually cast their ballot. Table 3.13 displays data in years since 1964 in which NES verified claims by respondents as to whether or not they actually voted. In only one year (1976) were women significantly less likely than men to have voted. In six of the eight years, although the differences were not statistically significant, men were somewhat

Table 3.13 Voters, Nonvoters, and Misreporters (NES)

		Said They Voted and Actually Voted	Said They Did Not Vote	Said They Voted but Did Not Vote	*p*-value
1964	Male	64.2%	21.0%	14.7%	.06
	Female	60.7	26.5	12.8	
1976	Male	62.4	23.6	14.0	< .00001
	Female	56.1	32.8	11.1	
1978	Male	40.9	45.0	14.1	ns
	Female	40.9	46.4	12.7	
1980	Male	60.7	28.3	10.9	ns
	Female	56.3	31.7	12.1	
1984	Male	62.1	26.7	11.2	ns
	Female	64.3	26.6	9.1	
1986	Male	41.8	48.1	10.2	ns
	Female	43.1	48.6	8.3	
1988	Male	61.1	28.8	10.1	ns
	Female	57.2	32.7	10.1	
1990	Male	39.9	51.3	8.7	.13
	Female	37.5	55.4	7.0	

Note: "ns" denotes not significant.

more likely than women to say they had voted when in fact they had not.

Even given the differences between NES and the Bureau of the Census, it is clear that the gender gap in voting that occurred before the mid-1970s has disappeared and perhaps even reversed. We now turn our attention to how this gender gap in voting behavior has manifested itself within different demographic subgroups as reported in data from the Bureau of the Census.

Voter Turnout Within Demographic Subgroups

Age. The gender gap in reported voter turnout is examined within the following age groups: 18–20, 21–24, 25–29, 30–34, 35–44, 45–54, 55–64, 65–74, and 75+.[35] For voters under forty-five, there was virtually no gender gap in reported turnout in the 1960s. In more recent years, women under forty-five said they had voted more often than men under forty-five. This gap among younger voters is larger than the gap in voting turnout between all men and all women.[36]

Among those over the age of fifty-five, men were more likely than women to say they had voted. This gender gap in reported voting has occurred throughout the thirty years of study and widens with each older age group (see Table 3.14). For example, among those between the ages of sixty-five and seventy-four, 67.0 percent of men and 61.3 percent of women said they had voted in 1994. This gap of –5.7 was larger than the overall gap in reported voting turnout for men and women in that year (0.6) but much smaller than the gap among those between the ages of 75 and 85 (67.0% of men said they had voted, compared with 55.6% of women; gap = 11.7).[37]

Table 3.14 Reported Voting Gap, Ages 65–74 Compared with Overall Gap

	A Reported Male Voting	B Reported Female Voting	C Gap (65–74)	D Overall Gap (all ages)	(D – C)
1964	77.4%	66.4%	–11.0	–4.9	6.1
1966	68.2	55.2	–13.0	–5.2	7.8
1968	76.9	67.2	–9.7	–3.8	5.9
1970	67.5	56.2	–11.3	–4.1	7.2
1972	73.1	64.3	–8.8	–2.1	6.7
1974	61.8	51.1	–10.7	–2.8	7.9
1976	70.9	63.0	–7.9	–0.8	7.1
1978	65.5	56.0	–9.5	–1.3	8.2
1980	72.7	66.7	–6.0	0.3	6.3
1982	67.9	62.4	–5.5	–0.4	5.1
1984	73.9	70.2	–3.7	1.9	5.6
1986	68.7	62.2	–6.5	0.3	6.8
1988	75.0	71.5	–3.5	1.8	5.3
1990	67.6	61.2	–6.4	0.7	7.1
1992	76.2	71.8	–4.4	2.1	6.5
1994	67.0	61.3	–5.7	0.6	6.3

Firebaugh and Chen (1995) believe that women socialized before the passage of the Nineteenth Amendment were less likely to vote than women socialized in later years. The stability of the gap between men and women in reported voting within age groups over the thirty years of data indicates otherwise. Women over the age of fifty-five report voting less, whereas the reported voting rate among men does not decline with age. In essence, there is an age effect and not a generational effect.

Race. The gender differences in voting behavior between white men and white women are similar to the differences found in the general population, because the majority of voters are white. Among blacks, the gender gap in reported voting behavior is consistently larger than among the general population. For example, in 1994 38.2 percent of black women and 35.5 percent of black men reported voting (gap = 2.7). This compares with a gender gap in the population of 0.6. This difference (2.7 – 0.6 = 2.1) remains fairly constant since 1964 (the average is 3.3).

Region. It is difficult to compare the gender gap in different regions of the country because the Bureau of the Census has changed its regional groupings over the years. However, we were able to compare the South with the rest of the country. Among southerners the gender gap in reported voting behavior was more pronounced before 1970 than it is today. For example, in 1964 61.4 percent of southern males said they voted, compared with 52.6% of southern females (gap = 8.8); this gender gap was larger than that for the entire population (4.9). By 1976, the gender gap in reported voting behavior in the South resembled the gender gap in voting behavior in the rest of the country.

Education. We examined the gender gap in reported voting behavior within six education groupings (0–8 years of school, 9–11, 12, 13–15, 16, and 17+) and found the following:

1. Among those with only an elementary school education (0–8 years), women said they voted at a far lower rate than men. For example, in that educational grouping, 26.1 percent of men and 20.5 percent of women reported voting in 1994 (gap = –5.6). This gap is larger than the overall gender gap in reported voting for that year (0.6). This difference (6.2) is fairly stable between 1964 and the present (average = 5.7).
2. Among those with a high school degree (12 years), the reverse holds true after 1972. For example, in 1994, 38.7 percent of men with a high school degree said they had voted, compared with 42.0 percent of women (gap = 3.3, compared with the overall gap of 0.6 in 1994; GD = 2.7). Again, this discrepancy is fairly constant over time (average GD = 3.3).
3. For those who attended some college or more (13 years and above), men and women reported voting at approximately the same rates.

Conclusions

The following three factors may contribute to the fact that women no longer vote at lower rates than men:

1. Women have increasingly entered the workforce over the last thirty years, which has broadened their horizons accordingly.

2. Women have closed the education gap with men, and people with more education are more likely to vote.
3. The gap in voting between southern men and women has closed.

Women as a Percentage of Voters

Even though women reported voting at lower rates than men in the years before 1984, they have still made up the majority of reported voters since the Bureau of the Census began asking about voting behavior in 1964, because there are more women than men in the voting-age population. Table 3.11 displays Census data on the proportion of reported voters who were women. Since 1964, this proportion has always been over 50 percent and grew slightly since then.

Recent exit polls also indicate that women make up a majority of voters. According to VNS exit poll data, women were a majority of voters in the 1990, 1992, and 1994 congressional elections (50.8%, 52.0%, and 51.2%, respectively) and in the 1992 presidential election (52.8%).

Notes

1. The times this will not be true are in races with more than two candidates or in polling prior to an election when the numbers do not add up to 100 percent because of "undecideds" or "no opinions."

2. With access to the raw data for NES, NORC, and VNS, we were able to do calculations to the nearest tenth of a decimal point and provide accurate *p*-values. The Roper Center and other survey organizations provided data rounded to the nearest whole number. In order to have consistency in the tables, all numbers were rounded off to the nearest whole number. However, the charts and most of the averages in the text are based upon the actual data. Therefore there may be minor inconsistencies between the numbers from NES, NORC, and VNS in the charts and text (rounded to the nearest whole number) and those displayed in the figures (rounded to the nearest tenth of a decimal point).

3. In *The American Voter,* Campbell, Converse, Miller, and Stokes (1960) noted that women were somewhat more likely than men to vote Republican in 1956. They believed that this occurred because women were older and less likely than men to vote in the Democratic South.

4. Researchers agree that in the 1950s women were more likely than men to identify themselves as Republicans. This gap reversed itself by 1980 as women became increasingly more likely than men to identify with the Democratic Party and to vote for Democratic candidates (Kenski, 1988; Cook and Wilcox, 1995; Bendyna and Lake, 1994). Other researchers (Wirls, 1986; Bolce, 1985; Bendyna and Lake, 1994) found that the gap in partisanship

widened during the 1980s as men defected from the Democratic Party to the Republican Party at higher rates than women.

5. Computing the averages based upon Table 3.1 would change the results slightly because numbers on the table displaying the average gender gaps since 1980 were rounded off to the nearest whole number.

6. NBC, CBS, and ABC joined together in 1990 to form VRS (Voter Research and Surveys)/VNS and did not conduct their own exit polls thereafter.

7. There are two major inconsistencies between the survey organizations: (1) In 1990, NES (gap = 10) shows a far greater gender gap than VNS (gap = 3); and (2) the reverse occurs in 1994, when VNS (gap = 11) shows a larger gender gap than either NES or Gallup (gaps = 4 and 6, respectively).

8. Because of the disagreement between NES and other surveys in 1978 and 1980, and because of the general lack of statistically significant differences between men and women with NES data, it is difficult to make accurate conclusions about the gender gap in those years.

9. The results of the various survey organizations are less consistent for party preference than for presidential and congressional voting. This is due in part to differences in the way the survey organizations ask people their party preference. For example, NES and NORC asked respondents who said "neither/no preference" when questioned about their party identification "if they felt closer to either party." "Leaners" who expressed a preference were then classified accordingly. Most other survey organizations code those who say "neither" as independents and don't attempt to determine if they lean. To make NES and NORC consistent with the other survey organizations, we classified NES and NORC leaners as independents. Classifying leaners into the appropriate parties when preferences were stated did not significantly change the results.

Some survey organizations changed the way they asked party preference from year to year. For example, before 1968, NES coded respondents who said they never vote as "apolitical." From 1968 on, these respondents were asked which way they leaned.

The *Los Angeles Times* used a seven-point-scale question similar to that used by NORC and NES in its telephone surveys. Exit poll respondents were asked only if they were Democrat, Republican, or independent. In some years respondents were given the option of choosing "don't think of yourself in that way."

Within and between survey organizations, there was also tremendous inconsistency with coding independents, others, people who said "don't know," and people who refused to answer.

10. For this example, the gap equals the percentage of women identifying themselves as Republican subtracted from the percentage of men who identify themselves as Republicans. The gender gap was computed in reverse of the normal method because there was little gap between men and women as to Democratic preference.

11. From 1952 to 1964, the average gap for independents was 4.5, according to Gallup. This is comparable to the 5.3 gap that NES found when respondents who stated "neither/no preference" were not asked which way they leaned. When NES asked respondents which way they leaned, the average gap for independents was far smaller—just 1.1. Women were more likely than men to say they leaned toward the Democratic Party when they initially had no preference.

12. One of the most significant gaps in U.S. voting behavior is the gap between African Americans and whites. The race gap in congressional elections has not been less than 30 points since 1962, with African Americans heavily favoring the Democratic candidates. The same pattern occurs in presidential elections. The last time the race gap in presidential elections was less than 30 points was 1960.

13. Party identification and self-identified political placement are not usually considered demographic variables. However, the differences are interesting to examine and it is useful to have the data for later analysis.

14. Some survey organizations show 1994 as having the largest gender gap since gender gaps have been measured, while others do not.

15. Other analysts have made the same point (Cook and Wilcox, 1995; Sapiro and Conover, 1993; Bennett, 1986; Miller, Hildreth, and Simmons, 1985; Paget, 1993). They note that the gender gap is complex and women certainly should not be construed as a monolithic voting bloc. Gurin (1985) gives four possible explanations for the lack of gender consciousness among women: Gender inequality is not as marked as other inequalities in the United States; both sexes jointly share in gains and losses as members of ethnic groups or economic classes; there is common socialization of men and women not only as husbands and wives but as brothers and sisters; and many women enjoy closer ties with men than they do with women and other associates outside the family.

16. If the GD exceeded 5 points, we ran a log-linear model of gender by vote by demographic category. The GD was considered statistically significant if a three-way model was required to fit the data. This process required approximately 400 log-linear models to be run with the NES data set. Because of the larger sample size of VNS, 5-point GDs were almost always statistically significant.

17. In analyzing the NES data in particular, we generally discount gender gaps in individual years that were different from other years. However, we did analyze a few isolated gender gaps that were exceptionally large. Extensive tables resulted from analysis of the NES data that are not displayed.

18. In general, there was a similar gender gap among all age groups in congressional elections between 1990 and 1994, according to VNS data. However, like Bendyna and Lake (1994) and Cook and Wilcox (1995), we found that in the 1992 presidential elections the gender gap for those under the age of thirty was somewhat greater than the overall gender gap (gap of 9.7 for those under the age of thirty, compared with 4.4 for all respondents; GD = 5.3).

NES data also show that in recent years the gender gap was not strongly influenced by age. However, as discussed in Chapter 6, among respondents under the age of thirty in 1960, women were far more likely than men to vote Democratic in both the presidential (gap = 10.8; GD = 16.2) and congressional (gap = 32.7; GD = 31.1) elections. For those over the age of sixty, men were far more likely than women to vote Democratic in presidential (gap = 25.2; GD = 19.8), and congressional (gap = 16.2; GD = 17.8) elections.

19. There was a tendency in both the VNS and NES data for the gender gap to be smaller than usual or reversed among lower-income groups in recent elections. However, these findings were rarely statistically significant and should not be overinterpreted.

20. NES data indicate that women in the North were more particularly likely to vote Democratic in congressional elections between 1962 and 1972 (average GD = 7.6) and in presidential elections between 1956 and 1972 (average GD = 6.8). It is interesting to note that the gender gaps in the South did not differ substantially from the gender gaps in the entire country.

21. Results from the NES data are complex. There was a pattern for the gender gap among liberals to be smaller (or even reverse) than the gender gap among the entire electorate in congressional elections since 1984 (average GD = 8.8) and in presidential elections since 1972 (average GD = 6.2).

Among conservatives, the gender gap was greater than usual in congressional elections between 1986 and 1990 (average GD = 5.7) and in the 1988 presidential election (GD = 6.3).

22. VNS did not ask respondents a question about their employment status in 1994.

23. A similar pattern is found in examination of presidential elections.

24. VNS does not ask questions about occupation.

25. Marital status did not affect the size of the gender gap using VNS data in the congressional elections of 1990. A full marital status question was not asked in 1994.

26. Kenski (1988), Bendyna and Lake (1994), and Cook and Wilcox (1995) found especially large gender gaps among professionals, those who were well educated, and those with large incomes.

27. See Cott (1995) for a discussion of how disunity among women before and after the passage of the Nineteenth Amendment precluded the development of a women's bloc.

28. Voter turnout is clearly linked to political participation. Sapiro (1984) examined women who were socialized prior to the advent of the modern women's liberation movement. She found that women who were interested in politics in high school remained so in later years. Education gave that interest an added boost. Marriage and motherhood also limited a woman's political participation. However, Sapiro was surprised that political participation was not affected by whether or not one was employed.

Schlozman, Burns, Verba, and Donahue (1995), using the Citizen Participation Study of 1989 (N = 15,000), found that men and women were very similar in terms of their political participation. They pointed out that one cannot simply lump together all men and all women. Participation differs according to race, class, and so on. In other research (1994) using the same data set, they found that situations in which men were more politically active than women usually occurred because men had more access to resources (jobs and income).

29. The Bureau of the Census asks questions on voting behavior every two years as part of the Current Population Survey. The CPS sample size in its election survey increased from approximately 35,000 households in 1964 to more than 70,000 in recent years. The NES survey is discussed in Appendix 1.

30. Campbell, Coverse, Miller, and Stokes (1960) noted in their pioneering study that in 1956 women were less likely than men to participate in politics. They expected these differences to dissipate as women became more educated and the older generation of women died out. Similarly, Verba, Nie, and Kim (1978) found that women participated less in politics than men in all seven countries they studied between 1966 and 1971. However, the participation gap was smallest in the United States.

31. Other researchers have also noted that the male-female gap in the voting rate narrowed substantially by the early 1980s (Welch and Secret, 1989; Cavanagh, 1981; and Baxter and Lansing, 1983). The lack of a gender gap in voter turnout has caused some academics to omit gender in models that attempt to predict voter turnout (Shaffer, 1981; Ragsdale and Rusk, 1993).

32. For example, in 1994 46.5 percent of the NES sample was male. NES does not weight its data to resemble the population data in terms of gender, race, or other characteristics.

33. For example, in 1994 60.4 percent of men claimed to have voted when asked by NES, compared with just 44.4 percent when asked by the Bureau of the Census (60.4 – 44.4 = 16.0). Similarly, 56.7 percent of women claimed to have voted when asked by NES, compared with 44.9 percent when asked by the census (56.7 – 44.9 = 11.8).

34. Hill and Hurley (1984) found that misreporters in 1976 were evenly divided between the sexes but that women were more likely to admit that they did not vote. Ragsdale and Rusk (1993) compared results from their 1990 Senate election study with voting data from the Bureau of the Census. They concluded that the lowest misreporting occurred among men. However, the Ragsdale and Rusk study did not examine whether the respondents actually voted.

35. The census used somewhat different age categories in some years.

36. For example, among those ages thirty to thirty-four, 58.5 percent of women and 53.6 percent of men said they voted in 1992 (gap = 4.9). This was larger than the gap in voting turnout between all men and all women for that year (2.1). This was fairly typical of all groups under the age of 45.

37. The gap was even greater among those over the age of eighty-five: 52.8 percent of men and 39.8 percent of women in that age group said they voted in 1994 (gap = 13.0).

4

Are Women Candidates as Likely to Win Elections as Male Candidates?

In 1995, seventy-eight years after Jeannette Rankin became the first woman to serve in the U.S. Congress, only 47[1] of the 435 members of the U.S. House were women.[2] Sixty-three years after the first woman was elected to the U.S. Senate, only 8 of its 100 members were women. Despite the fact that women began voting over seventy-five years ago and make up 51 percent of the population, just 8 percent of U.S. senators, 11 percent of U.S. House members, one governor, and 22 percent of state legislators were women in 1995.[3]

Since the early 1970s, women have been making slow but steady progress in increasing their numbers in elected offices, as Table 4.1 shows.

Why are there so few women in public office? The common perception has been that women candidates are less likely to win elections. A survey done in 1994 found that two-thirds of voters believe

Table 4.1 Percentages of Women in Elective Offices (Center for the American Woman and Politics [CAWP])

Level of Office	1975	1977	1979	1981	1983	1985	1987	1989	1991	1993	1995
U.S. Congress	4	4	3	4	4	5	5	5	6	10	10
Statewide elective	10	10	11	11	11	14	14	14	18	22	26
State legislatures	8	9	10	12	13	15	16	17	18	21	21
County governing boards	3	4	5	6	8	8	9	9	na	na	na
Mayors & municipal councils	4	8	10	10	na	14	na	na	na	na	na

Note: 1985 county governing board data are from 1984. 1989 county governing board data are from 1988. 1985 mayors & municipal councils data include Washington, D.C., and are incomplete for Ill., Ind., Ky., Mo., Pa., and Wis.

that women have a tougher time getting elected to public office than men do.[4] Several surveys have shown that even respondents who said they would vote for the female candidate predicted that the male candidate would win. Lacking adequate research, the media and political pundits have had to rely upon anecdotes and impressions to draw their conclusions. They speculated that more women aren't elected to public office because:

- The "good old boys" keep women from getting nominated for winnable seats
- Women just will not vote for women
- Voters cannot see women in top executive offices
- Women candidates cannot raise as much money

In politics, perception can become reality. A candidate's perceived ability to win an election can become a self-fulfilling prophecy. If a candidate is seen as less likely to win, he or she may attract fewer volunteers and supporters, have a harder time raising money, receive less attention from the media, and be less likely to receive endorsements from organizations and other politicians. This in turn may lead to fewer resources to run a successful campaign.

Then in 1992, the "Year of the Woman" in politics, women candidates were seen as having an advantage over men. Commentators offered several reasons for the supposed shift, including:

- Voters disliked political insiders and women are seen as the ultimate outsiders.
- The agenda shifted from the Cold War to domestic issues.
- The threat to reproductive choice energized pro-choice voters.
- The Anita Hill/Clarence Thomas hearings galvanized support for women candidates.

Is it true that women candidates are less likely to win than men? Or do women candidates now have an advantage at the polls? To answer these questions in an objective and quantifiable way, relying on statistics and facts rather than opinions, assumptions, or anecdotal evidence, we conducted a comprehensive study to compare the actual percentages of male and female candidates who won their elections.

The Study

Pollsters' questions, hypothetical match-ups, and sample studies can indicate how women might do as candidates. The real test, however, is how women actually do at the polls.

Our study compared the actual success rates of the men and women who were candidates in general elections for state legislature in 1986, 1988, 1990, 1992, and 1994 and for the U.S. House, U.S. Senate, and governor from 1972 to 1994. We also compared the success rates of men and women who were candidates in primary elections in 1994.

A massive data base[5] of 61,603 candidates[6] was compiled to make these comparisons. The data base included every major-party candidate—both male and female—across the country who ran in general elections for state house (a total of 40,436 candidates) and state senate (10,154 candidates) in 1986, 1988, 1990, 1992, and 1994, and for U.S. House (9,593 candidates), U.S. Senate (784 candidates), and governor (636 candidates) from 1972 through 1994. The following information was obtained and entered into the data base for each candidate: name; seat he or she was seeking; year; party; sex; whether he or she was running as an incumbent, challenger, or for an open seat; and whether he or she won or lost the election. Printouts of the data base were double-checked for accuracy. The Center for the American Woman and Politics (CAWP), which keeps lists of woman candidates, identified the sex of the candidates in this study. (Every "Kim," "Evelyn," and "Billy" was identified as male or female, a far more accurate method than a computer gender check.)

The year 1972 was chosen as the starting date for U.S. House, U.S. Senate, and gubernatorial races for several reasons. Prior to 1972, very few women ran for these seats; many who did run were widows following their husbands into office. In addition, 1972 represents the beginning of the modern era of women in politics, with the advent of today's women's movement and deliberate efforts by the National Women's Political Caucus (founded in 1971), the Women's Campaign Fund, and other groups to increase the number of women in public office. Since 1972, the number of women has tripled in the U.S. House and almost quadrupled in state legislatures.

For state legislative races, 1986 was chosen as the starting date because it is the first year for which CAWP has computerized records of every woman running for state house and state senate. Although fewer election cycles were covered for state legislative races, the number of candidates was large enough to yield results that are statistically reliable to a high degree.

Creating a complete file of state legislative candidates since 1986 was a daunting task. There is no central entity that keeps track of all candidates; each state keeps its own records. Few states include incumbency status on their election returns, so this information had to be obtained from other sources. And none of the election returns, either state or federal, includes the candidates' sex, so this information had to be added to the file separately.

Once the information on all 61,603 candidates was entered into the data base, success rates were calculated for each combination of year, party, incumbency status, and type of race (for example, male Republican incumbents running for state senate in 1988 or female Democratic challengers running for U.S. House in 1984). *Success rate* was defined as the percentage of candidates in each category who won their election (the number of winners divided by the total number of candidates).

Chi-square tests were run on the computer for every category to determine if differences found between success rates for men and women were statistically significant.[7] A small difference between men's and women's success rates might be statistically significant in a category with a great many candidates, whereas a larger difference between men's and women's success rates in a category with few candidates might not be statistically significant. For example, if three women run for governor, the success rate would be 33 percent if one wins and 67 percent if two win, but the difference is only one woman, and not statistically significant. On the other hand, if 1,000 women run for state house, the difference between a 33 percent success rate and a 67 percent success rate would be extremely significant.

The percentage of candidates in each category who were women was also calculated (the number of women candidates was divided by the total number of candidates). In addition, the study compared the percentage of male and female incumbent candidates for state house, state senate, and U.S. House who faced challengers in the general election.

To determine whether sex had an impact on success rates, the effects of sex had to be separated from the effects of incumbency. The study confirmed that incumbents win their races far more often than challengers or open seat candidates (candidates in races where no incumbent is running for re-election), and most incumbents are, of course, men. Therefore, female incumbents were compared with male incumbents, women running for open seats with men running for open seats, and female challengers with male challengers.

Additional comparisons were made according to party (comparing, for example, Republican men challengers to Republican women challengers) to remove any bias that might result from differences caused by party rather than sex. Results also were compared by year to find any differences over time.

State legislative candidates were divided by state and then by region of the country to look at possible geographic differences. The study also looked separately at legislative candidates who ran in multi-member and single-member districts.

The purpose of the study was to determine whether sex had an effect on candidates' success rates in general elections. In the process, however, a wealth of fascinating information unrelated to sex was revealed, including differences in success rates between Republicans and Democrats, differences in how often incumbents win their general elections for various levels of office, and the relative availability of open seat opportunities at various levels of office. (This information is included in the chapter section titled "Other Findings.")

The Findings

When women run, women win . . . as often as men do. Our study found no difference between success rates for men and women in general elections. Based on the overwhelming weight of the data gathered, the conclusion is clear: A candidate's sex does not affect his or her chances of winning an election.

Winning elections has nothing to do with the sex of the candidate, and everything to do with incumbency. The reason people may think that women are less likely to win is that most incumbents are men, and incumbents enjoy a huge advantage over challengers and open seat candidates. But when men running as incumbents were compared with women running as incumbents, men running for open seats with women running for open seats, and men running as challengers with women running as challengers, men had no advantage over women; women won as high a percentage of their races as men.

The percentage of women holding office at each level is strikingly similar to the percentage of women candidates who have sought each public office. From 1972 to 1994, 8 percent of the candidates for the U.S. House and U.S. Senate were women, and in 1995 women made up 11 percent of the House and 8 percent of the Senate. Since 1986, 21 percent of state legislative candidates have been women, and in 1995 women made up 22 percent of all state legislators.

Success Rates: State House and State Senate

The data base included 40,436 candidates for state house, among them 8,600 women, and 10,154 candidates for state senate, among them 1,760 women.[8] The large number of state legislative candidates allowed comparisons and conclusions that were statistically reliable by year and by party, as well as overall.

Table 4.2 illustrates the success rates for men and women who

Table 4.2 Summary of Success Rates, 1986–1994, State Legislatures

	Men		Women	
State house				
Incumbents	93.8%	(16,011)	93.6%	(3,881)
Open seat candidates	53.0	(7,268)	52.2	(2,316)
Challengers	9.7	(8,557)	10.9	(2,403)
State senate				
Incumbents	92.2	(3,890)	90.1	(674)
Open seat candidates	54.9	(2,132)	55.8	(513)
Challengers*	11.6	(2,372)	15.2	(573)

Note: Numbers in parentheses are the number of races in each category.
* $p < .05$.

ran for state house and state senate in 1986, 1988, 1990, 1992 and 1994. Women did as well as men in state house races for each type of race: Incumbent women won 93.6 percent of their elections, compared with 93.8 percent for incumbent men; women running for open seats won 52.2 percent of their elections, compared with 53.0 percent for men; and women challengers won 10.9 percent of their elections, compared with 9.7 percent for men.[9] None of the differences was statistically significant.

The data for state senate show women doing as well as men or better: Incumbent women won 90.1 percent of their elections, compared with 92.2 percent for incumbent men; women running for open seats won 55.8 percent of their races, compared with 54.9 percent for men; and women challengers won 15.2 percent of their elections, compared with 11.6 percent for men. The higher success rate for female challengers was statistically significant; the other differences were not.

The data broken down by party (Democratic male incumbents compared with Democratic female incumbents, Republican men running for open seats compared with Republican women running for open seats, etc.) again showed that women candidates were at least as likely to win as men. For state house, the differences in success rates between men and women were all 3.2 points or less. For state senate, the differences were somewhat greater (the smaller number of candidates, particularly women, made the results more variable), but if anything, women did better than men.[10]

In addition, success rates were examined year by year to see if aggregating the data might be masking significant differences in one or more of the years studied. However, the similarity between success rates held true over the entire period; no dramatic exceptions or changes over time were found. Basically, sex was not a factor in success rates during the time period studied; women and men have virtually the same chances of winning general elections for state house and state senate.[11]

Legislative Races Between a Man and a Woman, Between Two Women, and Between Two Men. Success rates were also calculated separately for state house and state senate races in which women ran against men, as well as for races in which women ran against women and men ran against men, in general elections. For this analysis, candidates without opposition and those who ran in multimember districts (where more than one member is elected) were excluded.

Once again, women did at least as well as men, if not better. In state house races, women won 52.5 percent and men 47.4 percent of open seat races in which a woman faced a man. For the state senate, women won 50.9 percent and men 48.9 percent of open seat races between a man and a woman.

Women also did as well as or better than men when they were challengers. In state house races, men won 9.0 percent of their races against male incumbents and 9.7 percent of their races against female incumbents; women won 9.9 percent of their races against male incumbents and 11.2 percent of their races against female incumbents. In state senate races, women won 15.9 percent of their races against male incumbents and 13.2 percent of their races against female incumbents; men won 11.2 percent of their races against male incumbents and 13.2 percent of their races against female incumbents.

Success Rates: State Legislatures by Region and State. In addition to being compared for the country as a whole, success rates for state legislative seats (state house and state senate combined) were compared by region and by state. U.S. Census definitions were used for the regions.

In the comparisons by region, the only statistically significant differences were in New England and East North Central, where female incumbents and challengers did slightly better than their male counterparts. In New England, 94.2 percent of female incumbents won, compared with 91.8 percent of male incumbents, and 15.1 percent of female challengers won, compared with 11.3 percent of male challengers. In East North Central, 8.3 percent of female challengers won, compared with 5.9 percent of male challengers. Otherwise, men's and women's chances of winning were similar across the country.

State Legislatures and Multimember Districts. Ten states elect some of their state legislators in multi-member districts.[12] To compare how women fared in multi-member districts as opposed to single-member districts, a separate analysis was done, with the state legislative candidates divided into those who ran in multi-member districts and those who ran in single-member districts. For this analysis, state house and state senate candidates were combined.

Women running as incumbents fared relatively better in multi-member districts than in single-member districts. In multi-member districts, women incumbents won 93.4 percent of their races, compared with 90.4 percent for men. In single-member districts, women incumbents again won 92.9 percent of the time, but men won 94.0 percent. For open seat and challenger races, there was little difference in success rates for women and men.

The greatest difference between multi-member and single-member districts was that women made up a higher percentage of candidates in multi-member districts. This was true for each of the categories—incumbents, open seat candidates, and challengers—as well as overall. Overall, women made up 26.5 percent of candidates in multi-member districts and 19.3 percent of candidates in single-member districts. In multi-member districts, women were 26.9 percent of incumbents, 27.4 percent of open seat candidates, and 24.0 percent of challengers. In single-member districts, they composed 17.2 percent of incumbent candidates, 21.8 percent of open seat candidates, and 21.1 percent of challengers.[13]

Success Rates: U.S. House

The data base had 9,593 general election candidates for the U.S. House of Representatives, 746 of whom were women.[14] Once again, success rates were extremely similar for men and women (see Table 4.3). Incumbent women won 93.6 percent of their races, compared with 94.8 percent for incumbent men; women running for open seats won 47.9 percent of the time, compared with 51.2 percent for men; and women challengers won 4.0 percent of their races, compared with 6.2 percent for men. None of the differences was statistically significant.

The data broken down according to party yielded similar results. For incumbents, Republican women did better compared with men than did Democratic women. For open seats, Republican women did somewhat worse than their Democratic counterparts. (Please note that the number of women in these categories is quite small.[15])

Table 4.3 Summary of Success Rates, 1972–1994, U.S. House

	Men		Women	
U.S. House				
Incumbents	94.8%	(4,315)	93.6%	(233)
Open seat candidates	51.2	(1,023)	47.9	(117)
Challengers	6.2	(3,509)	4.0	(396)

Note: Numbers in parentheses are the number of races in each category.

Similarly, there were no significant trends over time. For incumbents and challengers, men's and women's success rates were quite close over the entire twenty-two years. For open seat candidates, the small number of women running in any given year made the rates erratic, but there was no long-range trend. In sum, there is no evidence that women candidates did worse than men in general elections for the U.S. House.[16]

Success Rates: U.S. Senate and Governor

The picture for U.S. Senate and governor is less clear-cut because so few women have run for these offices (see Table 4.4). Since 1972, only sixty-two women have run in general elections for the U.S. Senate (two-thirds of them as challengers) and only forty-two have run for governor. In most of the categories of types of races, women did worse than men. However, each of these categories included very few women, and because of the small sample sizes, none of the results was statistically significant. Therefore, the only conclusion is that there is no statistically significant evidence that women are less likely than men to win general elections for U.S. Senate or governor.

Incumbent Opposition

Women incumbents running for re-election to state house, state senate, and U.S. House had opposition more frequently than men did. For state house, 66.9 percent of female state house members had major party opposition in the general election, compared with 61.4 percent of male state house members. For state senate, 74.3 percent of female state senators and 64.7 percent of male state senators had general election opposition. For the U.S. House, 93.6 percent of female incumbents were challenged in the general election, compared with 85.6 percent of male incumbents.

Female incumbents may be perceived as more vulnerable than male incumbents (whether because of their length of time in office,

Table 4.4 Summary of Success Rates, 1972–1994, Statewide Offices

	Men		Women	
U.S. Senate				
Incumbents	83.1%	(307)	71.4%	(7)
Open Seat Candidates	50.3	(149)	50.0	(14)
Challengers*	19.9	(266)	2.4	(41)
Governor				
Incumbents	78.4%	(171)	60.0%	(5)
Open Seat Candidates	50.4	(262)	30.4	(23)
Challengers	23.0	(161)	14.3	(14)

Note: Numbers in parentheses are the number of races in each category.
* $p < .05$.

the political makeup of their district, their sex, or other reasons); however, they have won as frequently as male incumbents. When success rates for incumbents who had opposition were compared, women did about as well as men at all three levels—state house, state senate, and U.S. House. For state house, the success rate was 90.4 percent for women and 90.0 percent for men; for state senate, 86.6 percent for women and 88.0 percent for men; for U.S. House, 93.1 percent for women and 93.9 percent for men. (There were not enough cases of women running for re-election for governor or U.S. Senate to do a similar analysis for those offices.)

The Year of the Woman?

Women's success rates were extremely similar to men's over all the years covered in this study; even in 1992, the so-called Year of the Woman, success rates were no different. Women won no more often than men in 1992, just as they had won no less often than men in previous years.

More women were elected to the U.S. House in 1992 because of two factors. The first was the record high percentage of open seat candidates who were women: 29.5 percent of Democratic open seat candidates and 15.1 percent of Republican open seat candidates. Twenty-two of the twenty-four new women elected to the U.S. House in 1992 won in open seat races. The second factor was a great increase in the availability of open seats in the U.S. House, which was due to redistricting, retirements, and resignations. A record high 21.1 percent of those who won U.S. House seats in 1992 won them in open seat races.[17]

Observations

Voters may be ahead of political pundits and the media in being able to look past sex to consider a candidate on his or her own merits and characteristics. While some voters may tell pollsters they are less (or more) likely to vote for a woman "all other things being equal," all other things are never equal. When it comes down to an actual choice in a voting booth, it is no longer a generic man versus a generic woman, but rather a specific man or woman, with specific views and experience and issue positions, from a specific party and region and racial background, running a specific kind of campaign against a specific opponent. Sex is but one of many factors that enter into the choice.

The fact that women win as often as men does not mean that voters see no difference between men and women candidates, or that their candidacies are necessarily the same. Surveys show that women candidates are assumed to be better or worse than men on certain issues and to have different characteristics just because they are women. For example, voters assume that women are more honest and caring, are better able to handle issues such as education and health care, and are weaker on defense and crime.

Women may encounter different obstacles in their campaigns, be treated differently by the media, or have to work harder (or less hard) to win their elections. They may win their votes in different places or from different groups of people. There may be a group of people who don't want to vote for a woman, balanced by a group of people who would prefer to do so. This study does not address any of these issues, nor does it suggest that the sex of candidates does not play a role in their campaigns.

Lack of Women Candidates

Our research clearly shows that women do as well as men in general elections. It also shows that the reason there aren't more women in public office is that not many women have run. Women have made up a very small percentage of candidates in general elections, particularly at higher levels of office.

From 1972 to 1994, only 7.8 percent of candidates for the U.S. House, 7.9 percent of the candidates for the U.S. Senate, and 6.6 percent of gubernatorial candidates were women. From 1986 to 1994, just 21.3 percent of state house and 17.3 percent of state senate candidates were women. These percentages are strikingly similar to the percentage of officeholders in 1995 who were women. In 1995, women made up only 11 percent of U.S. House members, 8 percent of U.S. Senators, 22 percent of state representatives, and 17 percent of state senators.

Women don't have a choice as to whether to run as incumbents; one has to win as a challenger or open seat candidate before being able to run as an incumbent. But women are not taking advantage of enough open seat opportunities to make up for the disparity in incumbency. For the years studied, women were candidates in less than one-fourth of open state house races, one-fifth of open state senate races, 10.3 percent of open U.S. House races, 8.6 percent of open U.S. Senate races, and 8.1 percent of open seat candidacies for governor.

Over time, the percentage of women candidates has been increasing steadily, although certainly not by leaps and bounds. For the U.S. House, 4.0 percent of the candidates were women in 1972 compared with 13.8 percent in 1994; for the U.S. Senate, 3.1 percent compared with 12.9 percent; and for governor, zero compared with 12.5 percent.

The similarity between the percentage of candidates who run for public office and the percentage of officeholders who are women offers great hope that encouraging more women to run for office will increase the number of women who hold office. If women continue to win at least as often as men do, more female candidates will mean more female officeholders.

Other Findings

Besides comparing the impact of sex on success rates, the study looked at other factors influencing the outcome of elections. The same data base of candidates running in general elections for state legislature from 1986 to 1994 and for U.S. House, U.S. Senate, and governor from 1972 to 1994 was used.

The Impact of Incumbency on Success Rates

Whereas sex has little impact on success rates, incumbency has an enormous effect. Incumbents win elections far more often than challengers and candidates for open seats.

A huge disparity was found between success rates for incumbents and challengers. In general elections for the U.S. House, incumbents won more than sixteen times as often as challengers; for state house, more than nine times as often; for state senate, almost eight times; for U.S. Senate, more than four times; and for governor, more than three times. Any minor differences between men and women were vastly overshadowed by the powerful differences between incumbents and challengers.

Members of the U.S. House had the highest success rate (94.7 percent) of any incumbents. Sitting state representatives and state senators won almost as frequently (93.8 percent and 91.9 percent, respectively), U.S. senators won 82.8 percent of their re-election bids, and incumbent governors won 77.8 percent of their races.

Most incumbent officeholders, at every level of office, are men, and a higher percentage of male candidates than female candidates are incumbents. Almost half of the men who ran for U.S. House were incumbents, compared with less than one-third of the women. Among U.S. Senate candidates, 42.5 percent of the men were incumbents, as opposed to only 11.3 percent of the women.

The fact that a greater percentage of male candidates are incumbents, combined with the fact that incumbents have much higher success rates, means that if male candidates are compared with female candidates without considering incumbency, men do better. This may explain the common perception that women have a tougher time winning office. Women do win less often, not because they are women, but because they are less often incumbents.

Open Seat Opportunities

Candidates for open seats win much more often than challengers, although not as often as incumbents. For the years studied, open seat candidates were anywhere from two to nine times as likely to win as challengers were. Non-incumbent candidates—men or women—who want to win would do well to look for open seat opportunities instead of challenging incumbents.

Open seat opportunities arise with varying frequency at various levels of office. As might be expected, the highest percentage of seats won in open seat races was for the office of governor, where term limits prevent many incumbents from running for re-election.[18] In terms of the percentage of open seat opportunities available, the office of governor is the most "open" to non-incumbents. In general elections between 1972 and 1994, 44.1 percent of those elected governor won in open seat races. The state senate is the next most open level (about one in four winners won in open seat races). State house and U.S. Senate were next (about one in five), and the U.S. House is the least open (about one in ten).

A similar pattern was found when challengers were added to the equation. Open seat candidates plus challengers made up 56.5 percent of the winners for governor, and only 15.9 percent of U.S. House winners.[19]

Party Differences

Women made up a greater percentage of Democratic candidates than of Republican candidates in this study at every level of office.[20] A greater percentage of women officeholders are Democratic as well. In 1994, 61 percent of female state legislators, 74 percent of women in the U.S. House, 71 percent of women in the U.S. Senate, and 75 percent of women governors were Democrats. By comparison, 58 percent of male state legislators, 57 percent of men in the U.S. House, 55 percent of men in the U.S. Senate, and 57 percent of male governors were Democrats.

If the patterns uncovered in this study persist, then the preponderance of Democrats among women officeholders will not only continue but will grow larger. Women made up a greater percentage of "new," or non-incumbent, candidates for state house, state senate, and U.S. House for Democrats than for Republicans in almost every election covered in this study. (There were not enough female candidates for U.S. Senate and governor to do a similar analysis.) By 1994, women made up almost one-third of Democratic non-incumbent candidates for state legislatures and more than one-fifth of Democratic non-incumbent candidates for the U.S. House.

The data base was also used to compare success rates by party, without regard to sex. Democratic candidates did better than Republican candidates at almost every level of office for every type of race: Democratic incumbents won more often than Republican incumbents, Democrats running for open seats won more often than Republicans running for open seats, and Democratic challengers won more often than Republican challengers.[21]

Primary Elections

After the National Women's Political Caucus released the study (Newman, 1994) showing that men's and women's success rates in general elections were virtually identical, a number of people who could not quite accept the results insisted that women must have a tougher time winning primary elections. They suggested that good old boys or the electoral system or voters who don't want to elect women must block women from getting on the ballots for general elections.

It would be extremely difficult to conduct a comprehensive study that included all candidates in primary elections for the state legislature. One problem is the sheer number of candidates who run in primaries; there are thousands of seats, and sometimes ten or more candidates run for each party's nomination. Another problem is the difficulty of obtaining the names and incumbency status of every candidate in every primary. A final problem is the near impossibility of determining accurately which candidates were men and which were women.

For those reasons, men's and women's success rates in primary elections were compared just for candidates on major-party ballots in U.S. House, U.S. Senate, and gubernatorial primaries in 1994 (1,964 candidates).[22] Once again, the perception that it is harder for women to win proved to be untrue (see Table 4.5). In fact, in the primaries studied, women were slightly more successful than men (although the differences were not statistically significant).

Table 4.5 Summary of Success Rates, 1994 Primaries

	Men		Women	
U.S. House				
Incumbents	98.8%	(325)	100.0%	(43)
Open Seat Candidates	41.8	(850)	48.2	(135)
Challengers	2.0	(149)	5.0	(20)
U.S. Senate				
Incumbents	100.0%	(23)	100.0%	(2)
Open Seat Candidates	31.0	(113)	31.8	(22)
Challengers	0	(21)	0.0	(3)
Governor				
Incumbents	90.9%	(22)	100.0%	(1)
Open Seat Candidates	24.0	(175)	26.9	(26)
Challengers	3.6	(28)	16.7	(6)

Note: Numbers in parentheses are the number of races in each category.

In U.S. House races, all 43 women incumbents won their primaries; 4 of the 325 men lost theirs. In open seat races, 48 percent of the women won, compared with 42 percent of the men. One of the 20 women challengers won (5%), compared with 3 of the 149 men (2%).

In U.S. Senate races, all of the incumbent senators, both women and men, won their primaries. Success rates for open seat candidates were virtually identical (32% for women, 31% for men). None of the women or men running as challengers won.

In gubernatorial races, the one woman incumbent running won (100%), while two of the twenty-two male incumbents were defeated (91%). Twenty-seven percent of the women and 24 percent of the men running as open seat candidates won their races. One of the six women (17%) running as challengers won, compared with one of the twenty-eight men (4%).

The results counter claims that it is harder for women to win executive offices such as governor than it is for them to win legislative offices. In fact, women were slightly more successful than men in winning primary races for governor in all three categories—incumbent, open seat, and challenger.

The same conclusions were reached when the races were divided according to party. The largest difference in men's and women's success rates occurred in U.S. House Democratic primaries in which no incumbent was running, where 52 percent of the women and only 39 percent of the men won.

In primaries, as in general elections, we found that only a small portion of the candidates were women. Women made up only 13 percent of the candidates in U.S. House and gubernatorial primaries, and only 15 percent in U.S. Senate primaries.

Conclusion: When Women Run, Women Win

The major reason there are so few women in public office is that there simply haven't been many women running for office—particularly for open seats, where the chances of winning are good. If women continue to make up fewer than one out of ten open seat candidates for higher office, or fewer than one out of four open seat state legislative candidates, it will take a long time to achieve parity. In order for women to win a sizeable number of public offices, a sizeable number of women must run—and this simply has not yet happened. Large increases in the number of well-qualified women running for winnable seats would significantly boost the number of women in public office.[23]

As mentioned earlier, the perception that women are less likely to win elections may make things harder for women, since candidates perceived as unlikely to win have a harder time gaining support and funding. The myth itself may have deterred women from making the decision to run for office. If women believe they are less likely to win, they will be less likely to try, particularly if it is true that women have a disproportionate "fear of failure."

Clearly, the prescription for greater progress in the future is to recruit more women to run for public office, particularly to recruit well-qualified women to run for winnable open seats. Women make up only a small portion of public officeholders not because they win less often than men, but because they have made up only a small portion of those running for office.

In addition, the U.S. political system is tremendously biased in favor of incumbents. In 1972 almost all incumbents were men, and incumbents are extremely difficult for anyone—man or woman—to defeat. Since at one time all officeholders were men, women did not start with a level playing field. Female candidates have faced the challenge of unseating sitting incumbents or have had to wait for incumbents to die, retire, or resign.

As long as most incumbents run for re-election and continue to enjoy huge advantages when they do, it will be difficult for any outsider—male or female—to win. Further research is needed on term limits, campaign finance reform, public financing, multi-member districts, cumulative voting, and other measures that might affect women candidates by diluting the tremendous advantages enjoyed by incumbents.

Perhaps women's progress is better than it seems to those who are impatient for faster gains. Women have been taking their places in public office at about the same rate as they have in business, law, and academia, if not somewhat faster. In business terms, the 535 members of the U.S. Congress could be compared to the CEOs of the Fortune 500 companies. There were fifty-five women in the U.S. Congress in 1995, and only one Fortune 500 company was headed by a woman.[24] Women hold only 6 percent of seats on boards of directors and 5 percent of senior management positions in the nation's largest companies.[25] Only 11 percent of partners in large law firms,[26] 15 percent of full professors,[27] and 9 percent of daily newspaper publishers[28] are women—rates that are comparable to the percentages found in politics. Women may be doing better in politics than they are in other fields.

Women entered the political arena relatively recently. Before 1920, women couldn't even vote. Very few women ran for public office between 1920 and 1972, and many of those who did were widows filling unexpired terms for dead husbands.

There has been a sea change in the involvement of women in politics over the past twenty-five years. Since 1972, the number of women has tripled in the U.S. House and almost quadrupled in state legislatures. As we see the results of the "pipeline" of women who have entered public office begin to pay off, and as women continue to become more powerful and prevalent in worlds outside the home, the numbers of women in public office will no doubt continue to rise.

This study proves that when women run, women win as often as men do. Perhaps this knowledge in itself will encourage more women to run for public office and lead to higher numbers of women officeholders in the future.

Notes

1. Plus D.C. Delegate Eleanor Holmes Norton.

2. The figures and many of the historical facts in this discussion and in Table 4.1 are derived from work done by the Center for the American Woman and Politics (1996).

3. Women served in public office even before the Nineteenth Amendment was passed in 1920. A woman was first elected to serve in a state legislature in Colorado in 1884. Jeannette Rankin (R-Mont.) served in the U.S. House from 1917 to 1919 and again from 1941 to 1942.

Most of the women who served in Congress before the 1970s were appointed to office when their husbands died or resigned. In 1922 Rebecca Latimer Felton (D-Ga.) became the first woman to serve as a U.S. senator; she was appointed to the office and held it for one day. The first woman elected to the U.S. Senate was Hattie Wyatt Caraway (D-Ark.), who was appointed to office after her husband's death and later won three elections, serving from 1931 to 1945. In 1978 Nancy Landon Kassebaum (R-Kans.) became the first woman elected to serve in the U.S. Senate without first having been appointed. Barbara Mikulski (D-Md.), elected to the Senate in 1986, was the first Democratic woman elected in her own right.

The first woman to serve as governor was Nellie Tayloe Ross (D-Wyo.), who served from 1925 to 1927. She won a special election to replace her deceased husband. In 1974 Ella Grasso (D-Conn.) became the first woman governor elected in her own right.

4. National survey of 1,000 voters conducted in July 1994 by Mellman, Lazarus, and Lake for the National Women's Political Caucus.

5. For the sake of consistency and comparability, the following guidelines were followed in creating this data base:

- Only candidates who ran in November general elections, not primaries or special elections held at other times of the year, were included.
- For state legislative candidates, only candidates who ran in general elections held in 1986, 1988, 1990, 1992, and 1994 were included. State legislative candidates who ran in elections held in odd-numbered years were not included.
- In order to have as large a data base of gubernatorial candidates as possible, candidates who ran for governor in general elections every year from 1972 to 1994 were included.
- For the U.S. House, only candidates for the 435 seats of voting members were included. Candidates from the District of Columbia and territories were not included.

- Nebraska's unicameral legislature was counted as a state senate. All state legislative candidates in Nebraska run as nonpartisans, and therefore were not included in the Republican and Democratic breakdowns.
- The goal of the study was to compare men and women as consistently as possible. After much debate, it was decided to drop Louisiana from the study for the sake of consistency and comparability. Louisiana does not hold "general elections" that are comparable to those of other states, and it was not possible to identify the "major party general election candidates" in a consistent or objective way. (For example, if one candidate wins over 50% in the primary in Louisiana, no general election is held; would all candidates who ran in the primary then be included in the study? All candidates can run regardless of party, with the chance for both a winner and a loser of the same party possibly skewing party data.)
- For U.S. House, U.S. Senate, and gubernatorial candidates, Congressional Quarterly's listings were used to determine incumbency. For state senate and state house, a candidate was considered to be an incumbent if he or she was listed as holding that office in the previous term in the State Elective Officials and the Legislatures books published by the Council of State Governments. A candidate running against an incumbent was considered to be a challenger. If there were no incumbents in the general election, the candidates were considered to be open seat candidates.
- For multi-member state legislative districts, non-incumbent candidates were considered to be challengers if the number of incumbents running in a district was equal to or greater than the number of winners to be elected from the district. If the number of incumbents running in a district was less than the number of winners to be elected from the district, the non-incumbent candidates were considered to be open seat candidates.
- Data for 1986 and 1988 state legislative candidates were obtained from the Inter-University Consortium for Political and Social Research in Ann Arbor, Michigan. Data for 1990, 1992, and 1994 state legislative candidates were obtained from individual state election returns collected by Election Data Services in Washington, D.C. Information on U.S. House, U.S. Senate, and gubernatorial candidates was based on election information published by Congressional Quarterly. None of the above data included the sex of the candidate, which was supplied by the Center for the American Woman and Politics.

6. An individual was counted as a candidate each time he or she ran for office in a general election.

7. Chi-square is a test of statistical significance that takes into account both the size of the sample (in this case, the number of men or women candidates in each category) and the relationship or difference that was found (in this case, the difference between success rates for men and women) and yields the probability (p-value) that the relationship or difference would have occurred by chance. If the probability is 5 percent or less, the relationship or difference is commonly considered by social scientists to be statistically significant.

For each category of candidate, a chi-square test was run. If there was a 5 percent or less probability that the difference between men's and women's success rates was a function of chance, then the difference was considered statistically significant.

8. The data base included candidates who ran for state house and state senate in general elections in 1986, 1988, 1990, 1992, and 1994. The following states did not have state legislative elections in one or more of those years:

Alabama:	No state house or senate elections in 1988 or 1992.
Kansas:	No state senate elections in 1986, 1990, or 1994.
Maryland:	No state house or senate elections in 1988 or 1992.
Michigan:	No state senate elections in 1988 or 1992.
Minnesota:	No state senate elections in 1988 or 1994.
Mississippi:	No state house or senate elections in 1986, 1988, 1990, or 1994.
Nebraska:	No state house elections in 1986, 1988, 1990, 1992, or 1994. (Unicameral legislature was counted as a state senate.)
New Jersey:	No state house or senate elections in 1986, 1988, 1990, 1992, or 1994. (State holds elections in odd years.)
New Mexico:	No state senate elections in 1986, 1990, or 1994.
South Carolina:	No state senate elections in 1986, 1990, or 1994.
Virginia:	No state house or senate elections in 1986, 1988, 1990, 1992, or 1994. (State holds elections in odd years.)

9. The percentage of incumbents who won added to the percentage of challengers who won does not equal 100 percent because the percentages refer to candidates, not races. Some of the incumbents ran unopposed, which means that a win by an incumbent does not always mean a loss by a challenger. In addition, in multi-member districts, a loss by an incumbent may result in a win by an open seat candidate. Further, some of the incumbents or winning challengers may not be major party candidates and are therefore not included in the percentages. For the same reasons, the percentage of open seat candidates who win is not exactly 50 percent. Some run unopposed, some are not major party candidates, and some run in multi-member districts against incumbents and a number of other open seat candidates.

10. See Table A2.1 in Appendix 2 for more precise data.

11. See Table A2.2 in Appendix 2 for more precise data.

12. The following ten states had multi-member legislative districts during the years covered by the study: Arizona, Indiana, Maryland, New Hampshire, North Carolina, North Dakota, South Dakota, Vermont, West Virginia, and Wyoming.

13. Whether the facts that women ran more often in multi-member districts, and that women incumbents were relatively slightly more successful, occurred because the districts were multi-member, or because of some other variable related to multi-member districts is beyond the scope of this study and warrants further analysis.

14. Note that candidates who ran in Louisiana are not included in this study.

15. See Table A2.3 in Appendix 2 for more precise data.

16. See Table A2.4 in Appendix 2 for more precise data.

17. See Table A2.5 in Appendix 2 for more precise data.

18. Some form of term limits for governor can be found in thirty-two states.

19. The U.S. Senate became the second most open level when challengers were included, because U.S. Senate challengers do relatively well compared with U.S. House and state legislative challengers. The percentages were as follows:

Open Seat Plus Challenger Winners as a Percent of Total Winners

State house	24.8%
State senate	30.3%
U.S. House	15.9%
U.S. Senate	34.3%
Governor	56.5%

20. See Table A2.6 in Appendix 2 for more precise data.

21. See Table A2.7 in Appendix 2 for more precise data.

22. The study included all candidates who ran in major party primaries as listed in *Congressional Quarterly.* Louisiana was excluded because it does not use a primary system comparable to that of the rest of the country. Delaware was also excluded, because no primaries were held for either U.S. House or U.S. Senate. For Virginia, only candidates who ran in the Republican second congressional district primary and Democratic U.S. Senate primary were included; all other nominees were chosen by convention.

An incumbent was defined as a candidate who presently holds the office being sought in the primary. A challenger was defined as anyone running in a major-party primary against an incumbent. An open seat candidate was defined as a candidate running in a major-party primary with no incumbent running in that party's primary.

23. An increase in the number of women running will not result in an increase in the number of women winning if the additional women who run have no chance of winning. If women run who are completely unqualified, have no ability to raise money or run successful campaigns, or are of the "wrong" party for their district, there will be little or no subsequent rise in the number of female winners. Interestingly, some women whose backgrounds are different from those of traditional male winners have been winning in recent years. Voters' definitions of well-qualified candidates and consequently the pool of potential well-qualified women candidates may be broader than in the past.

24. Source: Catalyst Inc.

25. Sources: Catalyst Inc. and *Fortune* magazine, September 1992.

26. Source: *Women in the American Workforce and Power Structure,* National Association for Female Executives, 1993.

27. Commission on Women in the Profession of the American Bar Association.

28. American Association of University Professors.

5

Do Women Vote for Women?

Do women vote for women? Is it true that women candidates have an advantage among women, that putting a woman on the ticket will help win women voters? Or is the opposite true—that women just will not vote for women?

The assumption is often made that women tend to vote for a woman candidate. It was widely assumed that by choosing Geraldine Ferraro as his running mate in 1984, Walter Mondale would gain among women voters. Speculation about New Jersey governor Christine Todd Whitman as a vice-presidential candidate in 1996 centered on the assumption that she would help Republicans win more women's votes. A television discussion of Mary Landrieu's 1995 campaign for governor of Louisiana included the remark that Landrieu "can't count on the women's vote because there's another woman in the race," which implied that she could have counted on "the women's vote" if she were the only woman (CNN, "Inside Politics," October 20, 1995).

On the other hand, a Democratic woman who lost her state senate race in a heavily Republican district and was disappointed at not winning a majority of women's votes wrote a book examining why "women won't support women running for office" (Henry, 1994). EMILY's List conducted a 1989 study based on discussions with women candidates and campaign managers that concluded: "Many women voters remained hesitant about supporting women candidates. . . . women voters did not provide a secure, early base for women candidates. . . . there is no 'leg up,' no advantage, with women voters." And it is ironic that the same Christine Todd Whitman who many said would help Republicans with women voters said of her own race for governor in 1993: "[Women need to] get the confidence to say . . . it's OK to come down on the side of the woman. I haven't been able to break down that barrier yet" (Borger, 1995).

The distinction between women voters and women candidates has frequently been blurred. For example, articles marking the seventy-fifth anniversary of women's suffrage often began by discussing women as voters and then continued with women as candidates, as though one necessarily meant the other.

This chapter explores the relationship between women voters and women candidates and examines in a quantifiable, objective manner whether women voters prefer women candidates, and if so, by how much.

Defining the Question

Do women vote for women? At the most basic level, the answer to that question is obviously yes. Women make up the majority of voters, and if women never voted for women, no woman would have ever won. Equally obviously, all women don't vote for women candidates; if they did, no man could ever have won against a woman. The real question is whether women voters give an extra edge to a woman candidate because she is a woman, and if so, how much of an edge.

To answer these questions, we began by comparing the percentage of women who voted for a woman candidate to the percentage of men who voted for that candidate. A woman might have received less than a majority of women's votes, for example, but if she received even fewer votes among men, she had an edge among women voters. Or alternatively, a woman might have received a majority of both women's and men's votes, but if her majority among women was larger than her majority among men, she again had an edge among women.

It is important to note that the existence of a gender gap in a race with a woman candidate does not necessarily say anything about women voting for women, because gender gaps occur in most races with or without women candidates. A gender gap has existed ever since exit polls have been able to detect it. Although sex is only one way to divide the electorate, and other divisions (such as race, income, religion, and marital status) are much greater (see Chapter 3), the gender gap has become a prevalent feature of political analysis. In the 1950s and 1960s, women tended to vote more Republican than men; since 1980, women have tended to vote more Democratic than men. One prominent pollster was quoted as saying, "You'll get [a gender gap] in a race for dogcatcher in Montana, if it's a Republican against a Democrat."[1]

To study whether women prefer a woman candidate because of her sex, it is necessary to separate out any preference by women for a woman candidate because of the candidate's party. If a Democratic woman did better among women than among men, it might not be because she was a woman but because she was a Democrat. To examine the impact of the candidate's sex, therefore, we compared the gender gap for women candidates to the gender gap for men candidates.

In most races between two men, the Democratic candidate does better among women than among men. Does this gender gap get bigger when the Democratic candidate is a woman? Normally, in races between two men, the Republican candidate does worse among women than among men. Does this gender gap shrink when the Republican candidate is a woman?

Methodology

Because election results are not tabulated or reported according to the sex of the voter, survey data must be used to compare the votes of men and women. To have a consistent series of polls, we used the Voter News Service (VNS) statewide polls for 1990, 1992, and 1994, which were conducted for almost all of the U.S. Senate and gubernatorial races in those years.[2] The polls were combined into a uniform data base that was analyzed in a number of different ways and for a number of different factors.

The data base consisted of 167 statewide races: 90 U.S. Senate races and 77 races for governor. Of these, 42, or about one-fourth, were races between a man and a woman; the rest were between two men. (There were no races between two women.) Only Democratic and Republican candidates were included in the study. The sample sizes for the polls ranged from 404 to 3,122, with most between 1,000 and 2,000 (error factor of ± 2–3%).

Of course it would be better to have more than 167 races to analyze, but VNS does not conduct exit polls for all U.S. House races, and private polls that are taken by candidates or the media in advance of races would not be consistent, objective, or reliable enough to use in research comparing various races. Although the study used the best data available, it is unfortunate that there were not more races to examine, particularly those involving women.

Findings

The Sex of the Candidate Affected the Gender Gap

• There was a gender gap in almost all of the 167 Senate and gubernatorial races in the study (see Table 5.1), with the percentage of women who voted Democratic as much as 15 points higher than the percentage of men who voted Democratic.

• For almost every year and type of race, the average gender gap grew by several points when the Democratic candidate was a woman, and shrank by several points when the Republican candidate was a woman.[3] Compared to races between two men, the tendency for women to vote more Democratic than men was greater when the Democratic candidate was a woman and smaller when the Republican candidate was a woman. This is the same as saying that the tendency for men to vote more Republican than women was greater when the Democratic candidate was a woman and smaller when the Republican candidate was a woman.

• In the ninety U.S. Senate races, the gender gap averaged 5.4 points in races between two men, 8.6 points in races between a Democratic woman and a Republican man, and 1.2 points in races between a Republican woman and a Democratic man. In the seventy-seven gubernatorial races, the gender gap averaged 4.8 points in races between two men, 8.2 points in races between a Democratic woman and a Republican man, and 1.4 points in races between a Republican woman and a Democratic man.

• In several cases when the Republican candidate was a woman, women voters voted more Republican than men voters did (creating a negative, or reverse, gender gap).

U.S. Senate

• In 1994 U.S. Senate races, there was an average gender gap of 7.9 points when both candidates were men (twenty-one races). When the Democratic candidate was a woman (two races), the average grew to 11.2 points; when the Republican candidate was a woman (four races), the average shrank to 3.0 points.

• The average gender gap in 1992 Senate races was 4.3 points when both candidates were men (twenty-three races), increased to 9.0 points when the Democratic candidate was a woman (ten races), and decreased to –5.6 points (in other words, women voted more Republican than men) in the one race in which the Republican candidate was a woman.

• In 1990 Senate races, the average gender gap when both candidates were men was 4.3 points (twenty-one races). When the

Table 5.1 Average Gender Gap in Various Types of Race

	Female Dem. v. Male Repub.		Male Dem. v. Male Repub.		Male Dem. v. Female Repub.	
U.S. Senate						
1994	11.2	(2)	7.9	(21)	3.0	(4)
1992	9.0	(10)	4.3	(23)	–5.6	(1)
1990	3.5	(2)	4.3	(21)	1.2	(6)
Total	8.6	(14)	5.4	(65)	1.2	(11)
Governor						
1994	7.3	(5)	6.6	(23)	9.0	(2)
1992	6.4	(2)	3.6	(9)	–2.7	(1)
1990	10.3	(4)	3.6	(28)	–2.3	(3)
Total	8.2	(11)	4.8	(60)	1.4	(6)

Notes: Gender gap is defined as women's vote for the Democratic candidate minus men's vote for the Democratic candidate.

Numbers in parentheses are the number of races in each category.

Democratic candidate was a woman, the gap was 3.5 (two races), and the gap was only 1.2 points when the Republican candidate was a woman (six races).

Governor

- In 1994 gubernatorial races, the average gender gap was 6.6 points when both candidates were men (twenty-three races) and increased to 7.3 points when the Democratic candidate was a woman (five races). In an exception to the general trend the study found, the average gender gap increased to 9.0 points when the Republican candidate was a woman, but this category was very small (only two races).
- In 1992 gubernatorial races, the average gender gap was 3.6 points when both candidates were men (nine races), increased to 6.4 points when the Democratic candidate was a woman (two races), and decreased to –2.7 points in the one race in which the Republican candidate was a woman.
- In 1990 gubernatorial races, the gender gap averaged 3.6 points when both candidates were men (twenty-eight races), grew to 10.3 points when the Democratic candidate was a woman (four races), and fell to –2.3 points when the Republican candidate was a woman (three races).

Did Women "Make the Difference" for Women?

- A gender gap was found in almost every race involving a woman candidate (just as it was in almost every race between two men). In some of these races, the woman won among both women and men voters; in others she lost among both women and men; and in still others, she won among one sex and lost among the other (see Table 5.2).
- In close races, the existence of a gender gap meant that the majority of women voters and the majority of men voters came down on opposite sides of the fence. When women voters support the winner, it is sometimes said that women "make the difference." If women made the difference in these races, then men made the difference in races in which they supported the winner. In races where the margin was not so narrow, the majority of women and men voted for the same candidate, even though there was a gender gap.
- In thirty-seven of the 167 races, one candidate won among women and the other candidate won among men. In thirteen of these thirty-seven, women supported the winner, or made the difference. In twenty-four of the thirty-seven, men supported the winner, or made the difference. In the 130 other races, the winner would have been the same even if only one sex had gone to the polls.
- Sometimes women made the difference for women candidates, and sometimes they did not. In twelve of the forty-two races in which a woman ran, one candidate won among women and the other among men. In five of these twelve races, women supported the woman who won; in five, men supported the man who won; and in two, women supported the man who won.

Conclusions

- The sex of the candidate did affect the gender gap.[4] On average, women have been slightly more likely than men to vote for women candidates. The average gender gap (tendency for women to vote more Democratic than men) was several points greater when the Democratic candidate was a woman and several points smaller when the Republican candidate was a woman than when both candidates were men. Relative to men voters, women voters have given a several-point advantage to women candidates in statewide races over the past several election cycles.
- All women did not support women candidates. Women candidates did not necessarily win among women, nor did they always do better among women than among men. On average, however, women supported women slightly more than men did.

Table 5.2 Races in Which One Candidate Won Among Women and the Other Among Men

	Vote Among Women (%, Dem. v. Rep.)	Vote Among Men (%, Dem. v. Rep.)
U.S. Senate		
1994		
Bob Carr v. Spencer Abraham	49.7 v. 46.1	36.1 v. 58.0
Ron Sims v. Slade Gorton	50.3 v. 49.7	38.4 v. 61.6
Dianne Feinstein v. Michael Huffington	52.6 v. 37.9	41.4 v. 52.0
Frank Lautenberg v. Garabed Haytaian	55.7 v. 40.8	44.5 v. 53.1
Ann Wynia v. Rod Grams	49.8 v. 44.4	38.7 v. 54.1
Charles Robb v. Oliver North	49.9 v. 39.0	40.4 v. 48.0
Jeff Bingaman v. Colin McMillan	58.6 v. 41.4	49.7 v. 50.3
Harris Wofford v. Rick Santorum	48.8 v. 47.1	45.6 v. 50.6
1992		
Les AuCoin v. Bob Packwood	55.8 v. 44.2	40.4 v. 59.6
Barbara Boxer v. Bruce Herschensohn	57.1 v. 37.0	43.3 v. 51.4
Lynn Yeakel v. Arlen Specter	53.7 v. 46.3	43.9 v. 56.1
Robert Abrams v. Alfonse D'Amato	53.4 v. 46.6	44.3 v. 55.7
Terry Sanford v. Lauch Faircloth	51.1 v. 48.9	44.4 v. 55.6
Wyche Fowler v. Paul Coverdell	52.1 v. 44.5	45.7 v. 51.4
John Rauh v. Judd Gregg	49.1 v. 49.0	45.4 v. 52.3
1990		
Harvey Gantt v. Jesse Helms	52.6 v. 47.3	42.2 v. 57.4
Bill Bradley v. Christine Whitman	53.5 v. 45.1	47.4 v. 50.8
Paul Wellstone v. Rudy Boschwitz	50.0 v. 48.8	47.7 v. 51.6
Governor		
1994		
Parris Glendening v. Ellen Sauerbrey	56.6 v. 43.4	43.8 v. 56.2
Larry EchoHawk v. Phil Batt	48.4 v. 48.1	38.9 v. 56.6
Lawton Chiles v. Jeb Bush	54.8 v. 45.2	45.6 v. 54.4
Ann Richards v. George Bush	49.7 v. 49.3	40.9 v. 58.1
Eddie Basha v. Fife Symington	48.9 v. 48.2	40.2 v. 56.6
James Folsom v. Fob James	52.8 v. 47.2	45.5 v. 54.5
Mario Cuomo v. George Pataki	48.2 v. 45.9	42.0 v. 52.8
Bill Curry v. John Rowland	34.2 v. 33.2	31.0 v. 39.2
1992		
Dorothy Bradley v. Marc Racicot	50.6 v. 49.4	47.4 v. 52.6
1990		
Barbara Roberts v. Dave Frohnmayer	56.3 v. 29.1	38.1 v. 47.2
Dianne Feinstein v. Pete Wilson	53.8 v. 42.4	41.5 v. 54.6
Ann Richards v. Clayton Williams	55.0 v. 38.6	42.8 v. 53.4
Peter Welch v. Richard Snelling	51.1 v. 47.1	42.1 v. 55.7
Zell Miller v. Johnny Isakson	56.5 v. 41.1	48.4 v. 48.6
James Blanchard v. John Engler	51.0 v. 48.1	44.0 v. 54.8
Paul Hubbert v. Guy Hunt	50.2 v. 49.8	45.4 v. 54.4
Terry Goodard v. Fife Symington	51.1 v. 48.0	47.4 v. 50.8
Joseph Brennan v. John McKernan	47.1 v. 46.7	43.8 v. 49.4
Ben Nelson v. Kay Orr	48.5 v. 49.3	48.7 v. 48.6

Note: Percentages do not always add up to 100 because of rounding and because there were additional candidates in some races.

• Sometimes "women made the difference" for a woman candidate, and sometimes they made the difference for a man; sometimes men made the difference for a man. These differences occurred because in close races, the gender gap put women and men voters on opposite sides of the fence. In most races, the majority of women and men voted for the same candidate, and the winner would have been the same even if only one sex had gone to the polls.

Observations

• Women voters and women candidates are two different categories and need to be examined as such.

• Since women make up a majority of voters and are not a monolithic voting bloc, their votes are key to winning elections. If a hypothetical candidate runs 5 points ahead among women and 5 points behind among men, that candidate will win the election, because women make up more than half of the electorate.

• Democrats and women candidates should not take the votes of women for granted, nor should Republicans or men candidates write them off.

• Although the sex of the candidate did make a difference in the gender gap, there is no reliable way[5] to determine if there was a difference because women moved toward women candidates, men moved away from women candidates, or some combination of the two.

• Women running for office should analyze and target voters according to a number of demographic factors: race, income level, religion, education, marital status, etc. The sex of the voter should be one of the factors, although it may not be the most telling or instructive. To win a majority of votes, a candidate must go after those voters whom she is most likely to persuade, and then make sure her supporters get out to vote.

Notes

1. Celinda Lake, quoted in Edsall (1995).
2. VNS was called VRS (Voter Research & Surveys) in 1990 and 1992.
3. Detailed tables on whether women are more likely to vote for women candidates are found in Appendix 3.
4. For purposes of comparison, and because other gaps such as the marriage gap, income gap, and race gap are larger than the gender gap (see Chapter 3), the study also calculated the average marriage gap and average race gap for races with and without women running but found no dis-

cernible pattern. In other words, although the sex of the candidate did affect the gender gap, it did not affect the race gap or the marriage gap.

5. The only way to test such a hypothesis would be to have two otherwise identical candidates, one a man and one a woman, running in the exact same race, and then conduct exit polls comparing how men and women voted. This, of course, is impossible in real life. The question can be tested in theory by asking people how they would vote for hypothetical candidates, and various studies have attempted to do so, but the results are not necessarily reflective of how people actually vote.

6

A Multivariate Analysis of the Gender Gap

The gender gap is a fascinating phenomenon to study. As discussed in Chapter 3, when gender differences in voting behavior and party identification occurred in the 1950s, women were more likely than men to vote for Republican candidates and to identify with the Republican Party. This gender gap started to shift party lines in the 1960s. Since the early 1970s, women have been consistently more likely than men to vote for Democratic presidential and congressional candidates and to identify with the Democratic Party.

There are many demographic and attitudinal differences between men and women that could cause a gender gap (see Chapter 2). In order to determine which differences actually lead to the gender gap in voting, we analyzed eleven variables. Our analysis suggests that women were more likely than men to vote for the Republican Party in the 1950s because women were less likely than men to hold blue-collar and service occupations and people in those occupations were disproportionately likely to vote for Democratic candidates. Furthermore, a great proportion of women were homemakers, and homemakers tended to vote more Republican than did blue-collar workers.

Whereas occupation was a major factor in explaining the gender gap in the 1950s, views on government and the economy have been the major factors linked to the gender gap since women started voting more Democratic than men in the 1970s. Polling data show that women have been more likely than men to support a larger role for government and to have a negative assessment of the economy, and people who hold these views are more likely than other voters to vote Democratic.

How We Examine the Causes of the Gender Gap[1]

NES data were used to examine the gender gap in presidential elections in 1956, 1960, 1968, 1972, and 1980 to the present.[2] The gender gap was also examined in congressional elections in 1956, 1966, 1982, 1984, 1986, 1990, 1992, and 1994.

To analyze the gender gap in candidate and party preference, three multivariate techniques were used: log-linear modeling, logistic regression, and least squares regression.[3] These techniques test which of the attitudinal and demographic differences that occur between men and women account for the differences in candidate and party preference.

The gender gap was analyzed in terms of six demographic variables:[4]

1. Age: 18–29, 30–39, 40–49, 50–59, 60+
2. Education (six-point scale)
3. Race (black = 1, other = 0)
4. Occupation-employment: professional-managerial, clerical-sales, blue collar, homemaker
5. Marital status: married, never married, divorced-separated, widowed
6. Frequency of church attendance (weekly = 1, else = 0).[5]

The gap was also analyzed in terms of five attitudinal variables:[6]

1. Whether the government should guarantee jobs: "Some people feel that the government in Washington should see to it that every person has a job and a good standard of living. Others think the government should just let each person get ahead on his/their own. Where would you place yourself on this scale, or haven't you thought much about this?" (guarantee = 1, other = 0)

2. Whether the United States should be less interventionist abroad: "This country would be better off if we just stayed home and did not concern ourselves with problems in other parts of the world." (stay home = 1, else = 0)

3. Economic assessment: "What about the economy? Would you say that over the past year the nation's economy has gotten better, stayed the same, or gotten worse?"

4. Personal financial situation over the past year: "We are interested in how people are getting along financially these days. Would you say that you and your family are better off or worse off financially than you were a year ago?"

5. Women's rights: "Recently there has been a lot of talk about women's rights. Some people feel that women should have an equal role with men in running business, industry and government. Others feel that women's place is in the home. Where would you place yourself on this scale or haven't you thought much about this?" (seven-point scale)

The Gender Gap—Partially Explained[7]

Presidential Elections

1956 and 1960: In the 1950s homemakers and those holding professional/managerial or clerical/sales jobs tended to vote Republican. People in blue-collar/service jobs were more likely to vote Democratic. Our analysis suggests that women were more likely than men to vote Republican in the 1950s because most women were homemakers and most men held blue-collar jobs (see Tables 6.1 and 6.2).[8] In 1956, 64.5 percent of women were homemakers (by 1994, less than one-fifth were) and only 16.9 percent were blue-collar workers.[9] In comparison, 0.6 percent of men were homemakers and 64.8 percent held blue-collar jobs. When we controlled for occupation, the gender gap disappears in these years. Note that there is little difference in voting between homemakers and men and women in professional/managerial or sales/clerical occupations.

Table 6.1 Percentage of Men and Women in Various Occupational Categories and Democratic Vote by Occupation, 1956

	Men in Category	Women in Category	Democratic Vote for President	Democratic Vote for Congress
Professional/managerial	25.8%	7.3%	33.2%	48.9%
Clerical/sales	8.8	11.3	36.7	51.1
Blue collar/service	64.8	16.9	50.7	60.6
Homemakers	0.6	64.5	35.2	46.8

The 6-point gender gap (using NES data) in the 1960 presidential election was created largely by older women who voted against John F. Kennedy in support of Richard Nixon. A clear gender gap occurred only among voters over the age of sixty (54.1% v. 28.9%; gap = 25.2).[10]

Table 6.2 Percentage of Men and Women in Various Occupational Categories and Democratic Vote by Occupation, 1960

	Men in Category	Women in Category	Democratic Vote for President
Professional/managerial	23.8%	9.9%	41.9%
Clerical/sales	10.8	16.8	43.0
Blue collar/service	65.4	17.3	59.4
Homemakers	0.0	55.9	43.3

1964: NES data show no statistically significant gender gap (only 4 points) in the 1964 presidential election between Democrat Lyndon Johnson and Republican Barry Goldwater.

1968: There was no significant gender gap for Democrat Hubert Humphrey or Republican Richard Nixon in the 1968 presidential election. However, George Wallace did better among men than among women (14.8% of men v. 8.8% of women; gap = 6.0). None of the variables that we analyzed explained this gap.

1972: A gender gap of more than 6 points (McGovern v. Nixon) can be explained by the fact that more women than men believed the government should guarantee every person a job and a good standard of living, and those agreeing with this position were more likely to vote for McGovern.

1976: NES data show a gender gap of only 1 point in the 1976 presidential election between Democrat Jimmy Carter and Republican Gerald Ford.

1980: Women were more than 6 points more likely than men to prefer Democratic incumbent Jimmy Carter to Republican Ronald Reagan. This gender gap persisted even we controlled for all the possible variables.[11] As was the case with Governor Wallace, women disliked Reagan (or liked Carter, or men liked Reagan and disliked Carter) above and beyond any explanation provided by the variables included in the models. This analysis was not changed by the candidacy of independent John Anderson, who received roughly equal votes from men and women.

1984 and 1988: The large gender gaps found in the presidential elections of 1984 and 1988[12] can be explained by the fact that women in these years were more likely than men to believe that the government should guarantee every person a job and a good standard of living (see Table 6.3) and that the economy had gotten worse over the previous year (see Table 6.4). Men and women who agreed with these two positions were more likely to vote for the Democratic presidential candidates (Walter Mondale and Michael Dukakis) than for Republicans Ronald Reagan and George Bush (see Table 6.5).

Table 6.3 Government Guaranteed Jobs

Some people feel that the government in Washington should see to it that every person has a job and a good standard of living. Others think the government should just let each person get ahead on his/their own. Where would you place yourself on this scale, or haven't you thought much about this? (Percentage responding 1, 2, or 3 on a 7-point scale, with 1 representing most in favor of government guaranteed jobs)

	Jobs		
	Men	Women	Gap
1980	29.1%	31.8%	2.7
1982	24.2	32.8	8.6*
1984	29.7	36.6	6.9*
1986	25.7	27.7	0.4
1988	25.3	30.9	5.6*
1990	30.9	38.7	7.8*
1992	25.7	34.2	8.5*
1994	24.2	33.8	9.8*

* $p < .01$

Table 6.4 State of the Economy

What about the economy? Would you say that over the past year the nation's economy has gotten better, stayed the same, or gotten worse?

	Got Better			Stayed Same			Got Worse		
	Men	Women	Gap	Men	Women	Gap	Men	Women	Gap
1980	4.4%	3.2%	−1.2	13.7%	12.4%	−1.3	81.9%	84.4%	2.5
1982	14.9	9.4	−5.5	20.5	16.4	−4.1	64.5	74.1	9.6**
1984	51.3	35.9	−15.4	29.0	37.1	8.1	31.3	37.5	6.2**
1986	29.2	19.1	−10.1	39.5	43.4	3.9	31.3	37.5	6.2**
1988	25.9	13.4	−12.5	49.2	50.6	1.4	24.9	36.0	11.1**
1990	4.5	2.6	−1.9	20.7	23.6	2.9	74.8	73.7	−1.1*
1992	6.1	3.4	−2.7	26.2	20.3	−5.9	67.6	76.3	8.7**
1994	42.1	31.1	−11.0	36.3	38.3	2.0	21.5	30.7	9.2**

* $p < .05$
** $p < .01$

Table 6.5 Percentage Democratic Vote

	Government Guaranteed Jobs		Economy Performance Previous Year		
	Yes	No	Better	Same	Worse
Presidential					
1980	67.6%	35.4%	57.6%	70.6%	38.9%[a]
1984	64.9	33.9	20.4	47.5	79.4
1988	72.4	40.3	22.9	47.2	65.5
1992	80.7	50.4	18.3	37.6	68.2
Congressional					
1980	74.8%	47.5%	70.3%	68.9%	51.7%[a]
1982	74.5	52.7	36.5	47.1	64.3
1984	76.4	48.2	41.8	56.1	81.3
1986	73.0	57.3	49.8	61.1	66.1
1988	78.3	53.4	41.0	60.8	70.6
1990	77.0	59.1	57.1	62.8	64.8
1992	75.9	53.9	38.8	40.5	66.9
1994	65.1	40.2	50.0	42.8	42.5[a]

a. In these years, people who thought the economy was getting better were more likely than others to vote for the Democratic candidate. This was the reverse of other years.

1992: NES data indicate that Bill Clinton won office with the support of 52.4 percent of women and just 42.4 percent of men (gap = 10.0), while George Bush had almost identical support among men and women (34.7% of men and 33.1% of women; gap = 1.6).[13]

In 1992, as in 1972, the gender gap can be linked to responses to the question on government guarantee of jobs and a good standard of living. More women than men believed the government should guarantee every person a job and a good standard of living, and those agreeing with this position were more likely to vote for Democrat Bill Clinton than for Republican incumbent George Bush.[14]

The gender gap that occurred when voters chose Clinton or Bush can be accounted for by the variables discussed earlier. However, those variables do not explain why men were more likely than women to vote for independent candidate Ross Perot (22.9% of men v. 14.5% of women; gap = 8.4). Gender was one of the most important variables in predicting the support for Perot even after controlling for other variables in the analysis. As with George Wallace and Ronald Reagan, women disliked Perot more than men did (or men liked Perot more than women did) beyond any of the factors we were able to analyze.

Congressional Elections

In the 1966 congressional elections, a greater percentage of men than women supported Democrats (61.7% of men v. 53.3% of women; gap = 8.4). The gender gap in 1966 cannot be fully analyzed because NES did not ask respondents about government intervention in the economy, the United States' role abroad, employment status, or occupation. The gap was not explained by any of the variables we were able to analyze.[15]

Since 1982, women have been more likely than men to vote for Democratic congressional candidates.[16] With the exception of 1990, the gender gap can be explained by the same two factors as in the presidential races: (1) Women were more likely than men to support government intervention to guarantee jobs and a good standard of living; and (2) women were more likely than men to have a negative assessment of the performance of the economy over the previous year.

In 1990 the gap between men and women on the assessment of the economy was smaller than in previous years, but that question, together with the question on marital status, accounts for much of the gender gap.[17] In particular, men were more likely than women to be married (66.3% of men and 49.8% of women) and people who were married (42.3%) were more likely to vote Republican than were single people (25.0%).[18]

Party Identification

The eleven demographic and attitudinal variables were also analyzed to determine which could account for the difference in party identification (as opposed to voting behavior) between men and women.[19] Although the findings are somewhat different, they are consistent with the results obtained when examining presidential and congressional elections.

Although there wasn't a significant gender gap in voting in 1952 presidential or congressional elections according to NES, in that year women were more likely than men to identify themselves as Republicans. This gender gap in party identification appears to be related to education. Women were more likely than men to have at least a high school degree (41.8% of women compared with 34.6% of men), and those with at least a high school degree (44.0%) were more likely than those without a high school degree (29.7%) to identify with the Republican Party.[20]

The gender gap in party identification in 1956 was related to a different factor.[21] Women were more likely than men to identify with the Republican Party because they were less likely than men to be in blue-collar and service occupations, and people in such occupations were more likely to identify with the Democratic Party.[22]

Similar to findings about the gender gap in presidential and congressional elections, the gender gap in party identification in the nine election cycles between 1972 and 1988 occurred because (1) women were more likely than men to support government intervention to ensure jobs and a good standard of living; and (2) women were more likely than men to have a negative assessment of the performance of the economy over the previous year.

The gender gap in party identification in 1994 could not be fully explained by any of the variables we studied.[23]

In summary, the strongest predictors of voting behavior and party identification have been whether voters believed that the government "should see to it that every person has a job and a good standard of living" and their assessment of whether "over the past year the nation's economy has gotten better, stayed the same, or gotten worse."[24] Women have been more likely than men to vote Democratic because women have been more likely to support government policies ensuring a reasonable standard of living for all Americans and to have a negative assessment of the economy. Women are more likely than men to believe that Democrats can solve economic problems and to support government policies to make sure that the economic pie can be shared by all.[25]

Notes

1. See Appendix 4 for a discussion of methodological constraints.

2. As shown in a previous chapter, some surveys show gender gaps occurring in years when NES does not. However, it is possible to examine only gaps that occur in the data. Therefore, the gender gap was not explored in cases where the NES data do not show a gap, including the 1964 and 1976 presidential elections and some congressional elections.

3. For an explanation of log-linear modeling, logistic regression, and least squares regression, see Appendix 4.

4. These variables were chosen because they were found by previous researchers to be important (Miller, 1988; Cook and Wilcox, 1995) or they appeared to have an impact on attitudinal differences between men and women in our previous analyses.

Several variables were not included in this analysis. Party identification and a respondent's self-designation of his or her political ideology were not included because we wanted to see if the gender gap was affected by differences beyond general ideological identification. Men and women differ as to political identification, and clearly this would affect their voting behavior.

Similarly, a question on attitudes toward the "women's movement" was not included because the term has become an ideological label. Instead, we chose to use attitudes toward "women's rights." The term *women's movement* has become such a catchword that being pro–women's movement correlated extremely high with voting Democratic.

5. The question on church attendance was first asked in 1970.

6. The question on government intervention was asked between 1956 and 1968 as a yes/no question; it was revised in 1972 to implement a seven-point scale. The question on foreign policy has been asked since 1956. The question on personal finances was first asked in 1966, and the question in which respondents assessed the economy over the past year was first asked in 1980.

7. For each year in which statistically significant (or borderline) gender gaps occurred, at least two different logistic regressions were conducted:

- To determine if the gender gap was a function of other variables, the independent variables in the first set of stepwise regressions were the eleven listed variables and gender.
- To see if the gender gap was different according to a respondent's demographic characteristic or position on an issue, the second set of logistic regressions used the same eleven independent variables, gender, and an interaction term of each of the eleven variables by gender (twenty-three independent variables in all).

Given the above results, secondary logistic regressions and log-linear models were run to see under which conditions the gender gap would no longer be statistically significant and if three-way interactions with gender would prove to be of interest.

8. The results in this analysis are derived from complex statistical analyses. In this case, gender does not significantly improve the fit of log-linear models that include occupation and presidential vote (change in LR [Likelihood Chi-Square Ratio] = 0.02, DF [Degrees of Freedom] = 1) or occupation and congressional vote (change in LR = 0.13, DF = 1). In order not to unduly confuse the reader, the results are summarized in relatively simple language. The log-linear results can be found in Tables A4.1 and A4.2 in Appendix 4 and an example of the results of the logistic regressions can be found in Table A4.3 in Appendix 4.

9. In Chapter 2, we discuss the fact that over two-thirds of women were homemakers in 1952; in 1994 fewer than one-fifth were.

10. Adding an age x gender x vote interaction term improved the fit of a log-linear model that included occupation x vote and age x vote (change in LR = 18.71, DF = 5; $p < .01$). The age interaction also created an apparent education effect, older people generally have less education. After controlling for the age effect, the education effect was no longer statistically significant.

11. Men and women in 1980 held similar views on the economy and whether the government should guarantee jobs and a good standard of living.

12. There was a three-way interaction between gender, presidential vote, and occupation in the 1988 race between Republican George Bush and Democrat Michael Dukakis. The gender gap occurred only among those in white-collar occupations. Male and female blue-collar employees were equally likely to vote for Dukakis.

13. VNS exit poll data gave Clinton a gap of 4 points and Bush no gap at all.

14. Also in 1992, foreign policy had a stronger effect on voting behavior among males than among females. Of men who said the country would be better off if we stayed home, 78.7 percent voted for Clinton, compared with 49.6 percent of those who said the United States should stay involved in world affairs (difference = 29.1). The corresponding difference among women was smaller (68.7% v. 58.6%; difference = 10.1).

15. Race was an interesting factor in the 1966 congressional elections. White men were more likely than white women to vote Democratic (59.2% of white men v. 49.4% of white women; gap = 9.8). This was reversed among blacks: Black women were more likely than black men to vote Democratic (96.4% of black women v. 82.8% of black men; gap = 13.6).

16. According to NES data, the gender gaps in congressional voting exceeded 3 points between 1982 and 1986 but were not statistically significant. The gap in 1988 was under 1 point. Other surveys show somewhat larger gaps for these years, but the analysis could not be conducted using NES data since the gaps were so small.

17. Gender had a borderline significant effect after controlling for these two variables (change in LR = 3.70, DF = 1).

18. People who are married have been more likely than other people to vote Republican since 1978. This gap was greatest in the year 1990.

19. Because the NES party identification question uses a seven-point scale rather than a two- or three-point scale, least squares regression analysis was used rather than logistic regressions.

20. Gender was not statistically significant after education was introduced as the first variable in the regression equation ($p = .46$). In contrast to 1956, occupation (blue collar was a dummy variable) was not significant in 1952.

21. The gender gap in party identification was not analyzed in 1954 because most of the questions of interest were not asked.

22. In a stepwise regression, a dummy variable representing women was no longer statistically significant after a dummy variable was introduced representing a blue-collar occupation.

23. In addition to the two variables discussed above, the gender gaps in party identification in 1990 and 1992 also were affected by women being more likely than men to believe that "this country would be better off if we just stayed home and did not concern ourselves with problems in other parts of the world" (30.5% of women, compared with 22.0% of men in 1992). Those with more isolationist tendencies (59.1%) were more likely than internationalists (46.9%) to identify themselves as Democrats.

24. We found two other points of interest:

- Asking respondents whether women should have an equal role with men in running business, industry, and government or whether women should stay at home consistently helped to predict the gender gap in almost all years in which the question was asked. This was true in the analysis of both presidential and congressional voting and party identification (the average beta for the role of women was 0.09). However, this question was never sufficient by itself to explain the gender gap.
- Although issues that are often identified with the women's move-

ment, such as abortion and the Equal Rights Amendment, do not account for the gender gaps in voting and party identification, these issues do have an important influence on why both men and women vote Democratic or Republican (see Abramowitz, 1995). People who support women's rights are more likely to vote Democratic than those opposed to women's rights. As shown in Chapter 2 (Table 2.5), there has been increasing support for women having an equal role with men in business and government.

25. Most of those who have used multivariate techniques to analyze the gender gap agree that compassion, economic concerns, and military intervention are important variables in explaining the gender gap (Mansbridge, 1985; Miller, 1988; Gilens, 1988; and Cook and Wilcox, 1995). They also conclude that the gender gap was not influenced by feminist issues. Sapiro and Conover (1993) found that feminist consciousness has no effect on attitudes toward Bush or Clinton, but Perot supporters were more likely to be male and anti-feminist.

7

Epilogue: Women as Voters and Candidates in the 1996 Elections

The 1996 elections were one more demonstration of the themes discussed in this book. There were variations, as there always are when only one year is analyzed, but the basic results were consistent.

Despite the inflammatory rhetoric and misleading headlines, the gender gap in the recent elections was not a chasm, women did not flock back to the polls after staying home in 1994, and attempts by Bob Dole's campaign to close the gender gap may have hurt rather than helped him. Women's behavior and influence as voters, and the success they achieved as candidates, were similar to those found in elections for the past twenty-five years. Women continued to make up slightly more than half of the electorate, to vote somewhat more Democratic than men, and to make slow, steady progress in increasing their numbers in elected office.

Women as Candidates

Twenty-five years ago, there were thirteen women in the U.S. House, one woman in the U.S. Senate, and none in governors' mansions. In 1997, there are almost four times as many in the House—a record fifty-one (up from forty-eight in the 104th Congress), a record nine elected to the U.S. Senate, and two women governors (double the one who served in 1996). Although these increases are not as dramatic as those that occurred in 1992 (the so-called year of the woman, when a record number of women ran for the open seats that

---

Parts of this chapter are planned for publication by the Roper Center in *America at the Polls: 1996* (Storrs, CT: Roper Center).

resulted from redistricting and the check-kiting scandals that year), they represent the same kind of "slow steady progress" that has been made in other elections since the early 1970s and that has made it no longer an oddity to see a woman debating on the floor of the Senate or House.

Once again, this election showed that the reason there aren't more women in elected office is not that women have a tougher time winning elections than men, but that there have not been enough women running for winnable seats (see Table 7.1). Six of the forty-eight incumbent women in the U.S. House chose not to run for reelection in 1996, and another was defeated in her primary, so the tally was down to forty-one before the races even started.[1] Women comprised only 14 percent of U.S. House candidates in the general election, the same percentage as in 1994. They were 18 percent of the challengers (up from 13 percent in 1992 and 16 percent in 1994), but challengers generally win their elections only about 5 percent of the time. For open seats, which represent the level playing field where women have a real chance to make significant gains, only 15 percent of the candidates were women in 1996, down from 22 percent in 1992 and 16 percent in 1994. Women will never achieve parity in Congress if they continue to constitute such a small proportion of the contenders.

Actually, in light of the small numbers who ran, women's progress was impressive. The eleven new women who won seats in the U.S. House more than made up for the six female House members who retired and the two who were defeated. Two new women were elected to the U.S. Senate, which made up for Nancy Kassebaum's retirement and the defeat of Sheila Frahm, who had been appointed to fill Bob Dole's seat. Jeanne Shaheen will join Christine Todd Whitman as the nation's only women governors. The conclusion once again is that "when women run, women win," but the impediment to progress remains the small number of women running.

As was true in the earlier years analyzed in Chapter 4, there were no significant differences in 1996 between men and women's success rates in U.S. House races when female incumbents were compared to male incumbents, female challengers to male challengers, and women running for open seats to men running for open seats.[2] For U.S. House races, female incumbents won 97 percent of their races, compared with 94 percent for men; women challengers won 10 percent of the time compared with 5 percent for men; and women running for open seats won 36 percent of their races, compared with 52 percent for men (but there were only fourteen women in this category). None of the differences were statistically

Table 7.1 Percentage of Candidates Who Were Women, 1996

	U.S. House			U.S. Senate			Governors		
	Number of Women	Number of Candidates	Percentage	Number of Women	Number of Candidates	Percentage	Number of Women	Number of Candidates	Percentage
Incumbents									
All	39	366	10.7	0	20	0.0	0	7	0.0
Republican	14	203	6.9	0	13	0.0	0	3	0.0
Democrat	25	163	15.3	0	7	0.0	0	4	0.0
Open Seat									
All	14	96	14.6	5	26	19.2	3	8	37.5
Republican	5	48	10.4	2	13	15.4	1	4	25.0
Democrat	9	48	18.8	3	13	23.1	2	4	50.0
Challenger									
All	63	356	17.7	3	20	15.0	3	7	42.9
Republican	22	159	13.8	2	7	28.6	2	4	50.0
Democrat	41	197	20.8	1	13	7.7	1	3	33.3
Total	116	818	14.2	8	66	12.1	6	22	27.3
Republican	41	410	10.0	4	33	12.1	3	11	27.3
Democrat	75	408	18.4	4	33	12.1	3	11	27.3

Table 7.2 Summary of Success Rates, 1996, U.S. House

	Men			Women			All		
	Number of Winners	Number of Candidates	Percentage	Number of Winners	Number of Candidates	Percentage	Number of Winners	Number of Candidates	Percentage
Incumbents	308	327	94.2	38	39	97.4	346	366	94.5
Open Seat	43	82	52.4	5	14	35.7	48	96	50.0
Challengers	14	293	4.8	6	63	9.5	20	356	5.6
Total	365	702	52.0	49	116	42.2	414	818	50.6

Table 7.3 Summary of Success Rates by Party and Incumbency, 1996, U.S. House

	Men			Women			All		
	Number of Winners	Number of Candidates	Percentage	Number of Winners	Number of Candidates	Percentage	Number of Winners	Number of Candidates	Percentage
Incumbent									
Republican	173	189	91.5	13	14	92.9	186	203	91.6
Democrat	135	138	97.8	25	25	100.0	160	163	98.2
Open Seat									
Republican	24	43	55.8	2	5	40.0	26	48	54.2
Democrat	19	39	48.7	3	9	33.3	22	48	45.8
Challenger									
Republican	2	137	1.5	1	22	4.5	3	159	1.9
Democrat	12	156	7.7	5	41	12.2	17	197	8.6

Table 7.4 Summary of Success Rates, 1996, U.S. Senate

	Men			Women			All		
	Number of Winners	Number of Candidates	Percentage	Number of Winners	Number of Candidates	Percentage	Number of Winners	Number of Candidates	Percentage
Incumbents	19	20	95.0	0	0	—	19	20	95.0
Open Seat	12	21	57.1	1	5	20.0	13	26	50.0
Challengers	1	17	5.9	0	3	0.0	1	20	5.0
Total	32	58	55.2	1	8	12.5	33	66	50.0

Table 7.5 Summary of Success Rates by Party and Incumbency, 1996, U.S. Senate

	Men			Women			All		
	Number of Winners	Number of Candidates	Percentage	Number of Winners	Number of Candidates	Percentage	Number of Winners	Number of Candidates	Percentage
Incumbent									
Republican	12	13	92.3	0	0	—	12	13	92.3
Democrat	7	7	100.0	0	0	—	7	7	100.0
Open Seat									
Republican	8	11	72.7	1	2	50.0	9	13	69.2
Democrat	4	10	40.0	0	3	0.0	4	13	30.8
Challenger									
Republican	0	5	0.0	0	2	0.0	0	7	0.0
Democrat	1	12	8.3	0	1	0.0	1	13	7.7

Table 7.6 Summary of Success Rates, 1996, Governor

	Men			Women			All		
	Number of Winners	Number of Candidates	Percentage	Number of Winners	Number of Candidates	Percentage	Number of Winners	Number of Candidates	Percentage
Incumbents	7	7	100.0	0	0	—	7	7	100.0
Open Seat	3	5	60.0	1	3	33.3	4	8	50.0
Challengers	0	4	0.0	0	3	0.0	0	7	0.0
Total	10	16	62.5	1	6	16.7	11	22	50.0

Table 7.7 Summary of Success Rates by Party and Incumbency, 1996, Governor

	Men			Women			All		
	Number of Winners	Number of Candidates	Percentage	Number of Winners	Number of Candidates	Percentage	Number of Winners	Number of Candidates	Percentage
Incumbent									
Republican	3	3	100.0	0	0	—	3	3	100.0
Democrat	4	4	100.0	0	0	—	4	4	100.0
Open Seat									
Republican	1	3	33.3	0	1	0.0	1	4	25.0
Democrat	2	2	100.0	1	2	50.0	3	4	75.0
Challenger									
Republican	0	2	0.0	0	2	0.0	0	4	0.0
Democrat	0	2	0.0	0	1	0.0	0	3	0.0

significant. We did not repeat our exhaustive study of state legislative races for 1996.

Women as Voters

In the 1996 elections, women made up 52 percent of the electorate. Women have been the majority of voters in every election since 1964, and their turnout rate—or percent of those eligible who actually vote—has been higher than men's in every election since 1980.

As can be seen from the figures in Table 7.8, the pattern that women make up a slightly higher proportion of voters in presidential election years than in non-presidential years continued in 1996. But as can also be seen, the myth that women "stayed home from the polls" in 1994 is just that—a myth. The statement promulgated in 1996 that 16 million women who voted in 1992 did not vote in 1994, and the even more dramatic statement that 55 million eligible women did not vote in 1994, are technically true but extremely misleading. Large numbers of women who voted in 1992 did not do so in 1994, just as large numbers of men who voted in 1992 did not do so in 1994, because 1992 was a presidential election year and 1994 was not. Turnout is always much higher—for men as well as women—in presidential elections than in non-presidential elections.

Table 7.8 Percentage of Voters Who Were Women

Presidential Elections		Non-Presidential Elections	
1984	51%	1982	50%
1988	52%	1986	52%
1992	52%	1990	50%
1996	52%	1994	51%

Note: All figures in this table are from CBS/*New York Times* and Voter News Service (VNS) exit polls.

The number of women who voted in 1996 was higher than in 1994 because 1996 was a presidential election year. Despite the women's vote drives in 1996, and the push that was made to appeal to women and to encourage them to get out and vote, women continued to make up the same 52 percent they did in the 1988 and 1992 presidential elections.

Women Voting for Women

Our analysis of U.S. Senate races in 1990, 1992, and 1994 (Chapter 5), found that the sex of the candidate made a small difference in the size of the gender gap. No such relationship, however, was found in U.S. Senate races in 1996.[3] The gender gap—or difference between the way men and women voted—was related to the fact that women voters are more Democratic and less conservative than men, and not to whether the candidate was a woman. Putting a woman on the ticket did not necessarily win over women voters in 1996.

In 1996, the gender gap in U.S. Senate races did not get larger when the Democratic candidate was a woman nor shrink when a woman was the Republican candidate. The average gender gap in the twenty-five races in which a Democratic man faced a Republican man was 7.4 percentage points. In other words, on average the Democratic candidate did 7.4 points better with women voters than with men. The average gap in the five races in which the Democratic candidate was a woman and the Republican candidate a man was actually smaller—4.4 points; and in the four races in which the Democratic candidate was a man and the Republican candidate a woman, it was about the same—7.0 points. The assumption that women will tend to vote for a woman, and the linking of women candidates and women voters that is often made by the press and pundits, as though they are the same topic, remained a myth rather than reality in 1996.

Table 7.9 Gender Gap by Individual Race, 1996, Senator

Democratic Woman v. Republican Man

Gap (Points)	Democrat	Republican	State		%Dem.	%Rep.
9	Sally Thompson	Pat Roberts	KS	Women	39	59
				Men	30	66
9	Mary Landrieu	Louis Jenkins	LA	Women	54	45
				Men	45	55
7	Jill Docking	Sam Brownback	KS	Women	47	50
				Men	40	58
0	Kathy Karpan	Michael Enzi	WY	Women	42	53
				Men	42	55
–3	Theresa Obermeyer	Ted Stevens	AK	Women	14	70
				Men	17	72

4.4 points average gender gap

(continues)

Table 7.9 (continued)

Democratic Man v. Republican Woman

Gap (Points)	Democrat	Republican	State		%Dem.	%Rep.
11	Carl Levin	Ronna Romney	MI	Women	63	34
				Men	52	46
9	Joseph Brennan	Susan Collins	ME	Women	48	43
				Men	39	56
6	Jay Rockefeller	Betty Burks	WV	Women	79	20
				Men	73	26
2	Jack Reed	Nancy Mayer	RI	Women	65	35
				Men	63	36

7.0 points average gender gap

Democratic Man v. Republican Man

Gap (Points)	Democrat	Republican	State		%Dem.	%Rep.
16	Joseph Biden	Raymond Clatworthy	DE	Women	67	32
				Men	51	48
15	Max Cleland	Guy Millner	GA	Women	56	40
				Men	41	55
12	Walt Minnick	Larry Craig	ID	Women	46	51
				Men	34	63
12	Tim Johnson	Larry Pressler	SD	Women	57	42
				Men	45	54
11	Dick Swett	Robert Smith	NH	Women	52	44
				Men	41	53
9	John Kerry	William Weld	MA	Women	56	40
				Men	47	48
9	Paul Wellstone	Rudy Boschwitz	MN	Women	55	37
				Men	46	45
9	Harvey Gantt	Jesse Helms	NC	Women	50	49
				Men	41	58
9	Jim Boren	James Inhofe	OK	Women	44	53
				Men	35	63
8	Tom Strickland	Wayne Allard	CO	Women	50	48
				Men	42	54
8	Roger Bedford	Jeff Sessions	AL	Women	49	49
				Men	41	57
8	James Hunt	Thad Cochran	MS	Women	31	69
				Men	23	75
7	Tom Bruggere	Gordon Smith	OR	Women	51	45
				Men	44	53
6	Tom Harkin	Jim Ross Lightfoot	IA	Women	55	45
				Men	49	49
6	Richard Durbin	Albert Salvi	IL	Women	59	39
				Men	53	43
6	Max Baucus	Dennis Rehberg	MT	Women	52	40
				Men	46	50
6	Ben Nelson	Chuck Hagel	NE	Women	45	53
				Men	39	59
6	Houston Gordon	Fred Thompson	TN	Women	40	59
				Men	34	65

(continues)

Table 7.9 (continued)

Democratic Man v. Republican Man (continued)

Gap (Points)	Democrat	Republican	State		%Dem.	%Rep.
6	Victor Morales	Phil Gramm	TX	Women	46	53
				Men	40	58
5	Steven Beshear	Mitch McConnell	KY	Women	45	53
				Men	40	58
5	Mark Warner	John Warner	VA	Women	49	49
				Men	44	55
4	Winston Bryant	Tim Hutchinson	AR	Women	49	51
				Men	45	54
4	Elliot Springs Close	Strom Thurmond	SC	Women	45	51
				Men	41	56
0	Robert Torricelli	Dick Zimmer	NJ	Women	53	42
				Men	53	42
–1	Art Trujillo	Pete Domenici	NM	Women	29	65
				Men	30	64

7.4 points average gender gap

Note: Percentages do not always add up to 100 because of rounding and because there were additional candidates in some races.

The Gender Gap in 1996

It may be hard to believe after all the hype and dramatic headlines, but the gender gap in 1996—although very real and certainly significant—was not a chasm.[4] In fact, it was exactly the same size as in the 1980 election between Ronald Reagan and Jimmy Carter, and was much smaller than a number of other gaps that divide the electorate today. But a rare convergence of the interests of the press, pundits, and pollsters led to a contagious rash of front-page stories this past cycle about a political war between the sexes, portraying the gender gap as having reached such overwhelming proportions that it had become a veritable Grand Canyon.

A gender gap is very different from a lead among women. Bill Clinton benefited from a large lead among women in the 1996 election—a lead that was in fact slightly smaller than Ronald Reagan's lead among men in 1980. But just because a candidate has a large lead among voters of one sex does not mean he or she has a large gender gap; if the lead among the other sex were exactly the same size, there would be no gender gap at all.

During the stampede by the media, pollsters, and pundits in 1996 to make the gap appear as new and dramatic as possible, the definition used to measure it was changed to one that made it look twice as large as the traditional definition. In the past (and through-

Table 7.10 Gender Gap in Presidential Elections

	Men	Women	Gap (Points)
1996			
Clinton	43%	54%	11
Dole	44	38	–6
	–1	16	17
1992			
Clinton	41	45	4
Bush	38	38	0
	3	7	4
1988			
Dukakis	41	49	8
Bush	57	50	–7
	–16	–1	15
1984			
Mondale	37	44	7
Reagan	62	56	–6
	–25	–12	13
1980			
Carter	36	45	9
Reagan	55	47	–8
	–19	–2	17

Note: This table shows the gender gap according to both the traditional and the new definitions. The traditional gap is the first gap number (Democratic gap) and the new gap is the third gap number (a combined gap).

out this book), the gender gap has been defined as the difference between the *percentage of the vote* that a candidate received among women and the percentage of the vote he or she received among men. Over the last year, the pundits and press started defining it as the difference between the *margin of victory* that a candidate received among women and the margin of victory he or she received among men.

For example, in 1988 George Bush won 50 percent of women's votes and 57 percent of men's votes, resulting in a 7 point gender gap according to the traditional definition. However, his margin of victory was 1 point among women (50 to 49 percent) and 16 points among men (57 to 41 percent), so according to the new definition his gap would be the difference between 16 and 1, or 15 points.

Although the newer definition is as valid as the traditional one, it makes the size of the gap appear twice as large. Some of the false claims about record gender gaps and chasms may have stemmed from this change in definition. Either definition can correctly be used; what is important is that the same definition be used consistently when comparing various gender gaps over time, or when comparing the gender gap to other gaps; otherwise, one will be comparing apples with oranges.

In 1996 Bill Clinton won by 16 points among women but lost by 1 point among men, which the press defined as a gender gap of 17 points. In 1980 Ronald Reagan beat Jimmy Carter by 19 points among men and by only 2 points among women, for an identical gender gap of 17 points. These gender gaps are as large as any that have been measured over the last fifteen or twenty years, but are not out of line with other gaps in the period, as can be seen in Table 7.10.

It is not surprising, in light of the issues on which men and women differ, that the gender gap between Bill Clinton and Bob Dole was as large as any that have been measured. As discussed in Chapter 2, women are more likely than men to want a greater role for government in social services and to support policies that help the disadvantaged. The differences between Clinton and Dole on these issues were clear-cut.

As is obvious from the exit poll data, it is not necessary for a candidate to "close the gender gap" in order to win an election. Ronald Reagan won handily in 1980 with the same gender gap Bob Dole had in 1996. In 1988 George Bush did 7 points worse among women than among men and won the election; in 1992 he did equally as well with women as with men, and he lost.

As the old political cliché goes, all that matters is winning 50 percent of the vote plus one, and this applies whether the votes come from women or from men. Bob Dole needed to do 10 points better among women *and* 10 points better among men, in which case he would have won the election with numbers similar to Ronald Reagan's in 1980. Closing the gender gap would not necessarily have helped Dole; in fact, to the extent that his campaign targeted women over men, it may have been aiming at exactly those voters it was least likely to win over.

Women voters tend to vote more Democratic than men because fewer women are conservative; on average, more women believe in a greater role for government than men do, particularly on matters like education, Medicare, and the disadvantaged. Dole's anti-government, lower-taxes message was one that was more likely to attract men than women. No matter how many women he put on the podium at the convention in San Diego, or how well-liked his wife was, or how much he talked about his support of the Violence Against Women Act, he was not going to close the gender gap.

The gender gap has little to do with abortion or women's rights. It was the fact that Bob Dole was a Republican and that he was more conservative on social programs and government spending that caused him to do better among men than among women, and not his position on so-called women's issues. Candidates who focus on abortion, breast cancer, and spousal abuse as though women can not get beyond their own bodies have missed the point. In fact, men's and women's positions on abortion and women's rights are almost identical, and just as many women as men consider themselves pro-life.

As was the case in the presidential campaign, the gender gap in congressional races in 1996 was real and significant, but was not a chasm; in fact it was smaller than in 1994. Table 7.11 shows the gender gap in U.S. House elections since 1980, using the traditional definition of the gender gap (the percentage of women who voted Democratic minus the percentage of men who voted Democratic).

Table 7.11 Gender Gap in U.S. House Elections (percentage voting Democratic)

	Male	Female	Gap[a]
1980	49	55	6
1982	55	58	3
1984	48	54	6
1986	51	54	3
1988	52	57	5
1990	52	55	3
1992	52	55	3
1994	42	53	11
1996	45	54	9

a. This table shows the traditional definition of the gender gap, as used in the rest of the book. If the new definition were used, each gap would appear twice as large.

As can be seen, women have stayed remarkably consistent in their voting over the past sixteen years, with between 53 and 58 percent voting Democratic each year. Men's voting behavior has been more erratic, ranging from 42 to 55 percent Democratic. In fact, Table 7.11 shows quite clearly that it was men's dramatic shift to the right in 1994 that resulted in the victories of Newt Gingrich and the Republicans, rather than any apathy on the part of women.

The similarities in the way women and men vote are much greater than the differences. Most husbands vote the same way their wives do, despite the myth that couples go to the polls and cancel out each other's votes. However, although the gender gap is not a chasm, there are other gaps that do constitute chasms in the electorate today.

For example, whereas 54 percent of women voted for Clinton in 1996 versus only 43 percent of men, 84 percent of blacks voted for

Table 7.12 Gender Gap Versus Demographic Subgroup Gap, 1996, Presidential Election (VNS)

	Percentage Voting Democrat	Percentage Voting Republican	Percentage for Perot
Gender			
Male	43	44	7
Female	54	38	7
Largest Gap	11	6	0
Race			
White	44	46	8
Black	84	12	4
Largest Gap	40	34	4
Age			
18–29	53	35	10
30–44	49	41	8
45–59	47	43	8
60+	50	43	6
Largest Gap	6	8	4
Education			
Less HS	58	29	11
HS Grad	51	35	13
Some College	48	41	10
College Grad	43	48	7
Postgraduate	53	39	4
Largest Gap	15	19	9
Income			
Under $15,000	60	26	11
$15,000–$30,000	54	36	8
$30,000–$50,000	49	40	9
$50,000–$75,000	46	46	6
$75,000–$100,000	44	49	6
over $100,000	40	54	5
Largest Gap	20	28	6
Religion			
Protestant	41	50	8
Catholic	53	38	8
Other Christian	49	38	12
Jewish	80	16	3
Other	62	25	7
None	57	26	13
Largest Gap	39	34	10
Party Identification			
Democrat	84	10	5
Republican	13	81	5
Independent/Other	43	37	16
Largest Gap	71	71	11
Political Ideology			
Liberal	78	11	7
Moderate	57	33	9
Conservative	20	72	7
Largest Gap	58	61	2

him versus only 44 percent of whites (see Table 7.12). This is a true chasm. Clinton lost to Dole by 2 points among whites and won by 72 points among blacks, which would be a race gap of 74 points according to the new definition of a "gap." Similarly, 41 percent of Protestants voted for Clinton, compared with 80 percent of Jews (a gap of 73 points according to the new definition). Despite the current fascination with differences between men and women—the Mars/Venus phenomenon—it is more instructive to look at income, education, race, and religious and geographic differences that divide voters today than at differences between the sexes.

Women Are Crucial in Modern Elections

Women are crucial in elections today not because they vote as a bloc but because they make up more than half of the electorate. Misunderstanding the influence of women voters can only compound the problems caused by a misunderstanding of the gender gap.

Blacks and Jews are true voting blocs; women are not. Those who speak of "the women's vote" as though it is a special interest group or a homogeneous segment of voters are in danger of underestimating the diverse, influential majority of voters that women comprise. No Democratic candidate can afford to take women's votes for granted; no Republican can afford to lose too many. A force this powerful should not be surrounded by hyperbole and spin, but rather should be carefully understood and accurately interpreted.

Notes

1. Table 7.1 cites thirty-nine female incumbents. The difference is due to Representative Sheila Jackson Lee (D) and Representative Eddie Bernice Johnson (D) who ran in two of the thirteen Texas districts that were omitted from this analysis. See note 2 for more details.

2. In our analysis of women as candidates, we utilized the same methodology as described in Chapter 4. Because of peculiarities of the 1996 election the following decisions were made:

- We excluded thirteen districts from Texas because they held special elections on election day. The format of these special elections resembled those of Louisiana that we exclude in Chapter 4.
- Jo Ann Emerson (MO-08) was listed as a Republican candidate.

3. In our analysis of women voting for women, we utilized the same

methodology as described in Chapter 5. Throughout this book we generally exclude races from Louisiana because of the unique manner in which general elections are held in that state. We include Louisiana in this discussion because in the 1996 Louisiana senate election a Democrat faced a Republican, and because of the interest generated by the Landrieu candidacy.

4. We use data from VNS to compute the 1996 gender gap. The only other exit poll conducted in 1996 was by the *Los Angeles Times,* and the size of their gender gap was comparable with that of VNS (58% v. 45%; gap = 13). When we compare the gender gap with years before 1990 we use CBS/*New York Times* exit poll data.

Discrepancies will occur between the VNS results we display and VNS data released by other sources. VNS reweighs their data several times before issuing a final release several months after the election. Our gender gap data on the presidential election came from telephone conversations with staff at VNS in late December 1996. We took other VNS data from the Politics Now internet site. Politics Now is a joint service of ABC News, the *National Journal,* the *Washington Post,* the *Los Angeles Times,* and *Newsweek.* These data have not been updated since the day after the election.

Appendix 1: Introduction to the Data

We first learned how challenging it would be to study the gender gap in this country while researching a study for the National Women's Political Caucus.[1] For example, take a simple question such as, What percentage of voters are women? We found one article that said 52 percent, a report from a different source cited 53 percent, and a third said 51 percent. We came to realize that it was not inaccuracy we had encountered, but the vagueness of the question as well as the inexactness of political statistics.[2] Each of the numbers was accurate (given margins of error), depending on the election, the year, and, since election statistics are not reported by sex, how the data were derived—from exit polls, from Census Bureau data, or from other postelection surveys.

A similar problem arises when determining the number of people who are eligible to vote and the number who actually vote in any particular election. The figures commonly used for eligible voters are provided by the Census Bureau (derived from the Current Population Survey), which estimates how many Americans were eighteen years or older at the time of the election. These figures, however, include millions of non-citizens and convicted felons who are not eligible to vote, and they exclude Americans living abroad who are eligible to vote. Census Bureau data on the number of registered voters are based on the number of people who say they are registered, which can be quite unreliable. Even the numbers of registered voters supplied by state election officials are not accurate because up to 10 percent of people on registration lists have died or moved.

The actual number of people who vote in any given election is not measured in a uniform way. Some states release data on how many ballots were passed out; in other states, one must use the race that resulted in the highest number of votes. However, some voters don't cast ballots in all races and some ballots are disqualified. The number of people who actually vote is traditionally 5 to 15 percent lower than the number of people who tell the Census Bureau they vote.

An interesting example of the ambiguity of election statistics occurred after the 1994 elections. Curtis Gans (1995) of the Committee for the Study of the American Electorate analyzes voting patterns and releases a report after each election based on actual election results. Gans found actual turnout up in 1994 despite a general downward trend since the 1960s. He delayed releasing his report for two months to see if the Census Bureau report on the election would shed some light on which demographic groups could account for the increase. But when the Census Bureau survey came out, it showed reported turnout down slightly.

Words can be at least as ambiguous and controversial as data. For example, we debated about which word to use—*sex* or *gender.* Clearly, the term *gender gap* has become well known, and it wouldn't make sense to talk about a "sex gap." But *gender* is used by social scientists to refer to much more than whether a person is male or female (such as the expectations and roles that men and women play, society's attitudes toward the two sexes, and the different upbringing that girls and boys experience).

From a purist's point of view, this study is about sex, not gender. However, the word *gender* is being used increasingly as a substitute for the word *sex,* partly to avoid discomfort in using the latter word and to eliminate confusion with the other connotations and meanings it can have. In the words of one social scientist, "It is both unproductive and in violation of the original sense of the concept of 'gender' to talk about 'two genders' as a euphemism for 'two sexes.' But when Lands' End starts putting 'gender-F' on their clothing tags, I guess this battle is lost."[3] It would be pointless to try and rename the gender gap out of a sense of purism. Therefore, we have tried to use the word *sex* when possible but have used the term *gender* when appropriate.

Sources of Data (Chapters 2, 3, 5, 6)

A variety of data sources were used to study the attitudes and actions of voters.[4] Following are brief descriptions of each source and its associated advantages and disadvantages.

Voter News Service (VNS)

In 1990 four television networks (ABC, CBS, NBC, and CNN) created a consortium to conduct exit polls for that year's election. This organization was called Voter Research and Surveys (VRS) through the 1992 election cycle. In 1994 the Associated Press joined the consortium and it was renamed Voter News Service (VNS).[5] Typically, VNS stations interviewers outside polling places in randomly chosen precincts. Voters are chosen systematically throughout the voting day and asked to fill out a brief questionnaire. VNS conducted two types of surveys between 1990 and 1994:

- A national poll for each election cycle. The national poll's sample sizes are as follows:

1990	19,410
1992	15,365
1994	11,303

- A series of state polls for each election cycle. Sample sizes for the state polls are as follows:

1990	67,002	42 states
1992	54,806	51 states
1994	52,852	36 states

We combined the three national surveys into one data set using only common variables. Similarly, the 129 state surveys were combined into one data set.

The main advantages of VNS data are:

- Very large sample sizes allow for extensive breakdowns by demographic variables. For example, it is possible to make meaningful statements about black female voters under the age of twenty-nine.
- Large sample sizes for each state allow for analysis of individual U.S. Senate and gubernatorial races.
- Individuals are interviewed immediately after they vote.
- Because the interviewer can collect some information about those who refuse to be interviewed (sex, race, and age), it is easier to make imputations for those who refuse.

There are limitations with the data:

- The various surveys sometimes ask questions in different ways from year to year. For example, the age and income intervals differ across the years. For the most part, variables were created in which there were uniform coding categories.
- VNS data only go back to 1990. Therefore, it is impossible to

use VNS data to analyze long-term changes in voting behavior.
- The national data sets have insufficient sample sizes within each state to allow for detailed analysis of U.S. Senate and gubernatorial campaigns. One must therefore rely upon the state surveys.
- The state data sets did not ask how respondents voted in U.S. House races; therefore one must rely upon the national surveys. However, the national surveys do not sample from all congressional districts.[6]
- A typical exit poll takes just five minutes to complete, so VNS asks a very limited set of questions about political attitudes (abortion, gun control, etc.). In addition, many of the attitudinal questions are not asked from year to year. Consequently, it is difficult to consistently relate voting behavior to other political and social attitudes.

American National Election Studies (NES)

The American National Election Studies (NES) (Miller, 1994) is conducted by the Survey Research Center and Center for Political Studies of the Institute for Social Research at the University of Michigan. NES conducts surveys with 1,000 to 2,000 respondents every two years.[7] Households are chosen using a probability sample of citizens of voting age living in private households. For the most part, surveys are conducted face-to-face, last one to three hours, and are conducted shortly after the elections. NES has historically been the major source of data used by social scientists to examine voting behavior.

The advantages of NES data are:

- There are detailed questions about voting and political behavior.
- Many of the data series go back to 1952.

The disadvantages of NES data are:

- Although the sample size for any one year is comparable to most other surveys conducted face-to-face and by telephone, it is far smaller than many exit polls. Therefore, some of the detailed breaking down into demographic groups cannot be done as the subsample sizes become too small.
- NES asks few questions about social attitudes (relative to NORC). For example, whereas NORC has asked seven ques-

tions about abortion in every year since 1972, NES asked one question before 1980 and a somewhat different question after 1980.

- The phraseology of questions changes more frequently than with NORC.

National Opinion Research Center (NORC)

The National Opinion Research Center (NORC), which is associated with the University of Chicago (Davis and Smith, 1992, 1994), has conducted its General Social Survey (GSS) every year or every other year since 1972. The typical sample size is about 1,500. NORC's major goal is to facilitate trend studies in social attitudes. Therefore, careful attention is paid to having the same phraseology of questions from year to year and asking a large number of questions about political and social attitudes and behavior. NORC chooses households using a probability sample of citizens of voting age living in private households. Surveys are conducted face-to-face and last one to three hours. The NORC GSS is the survey most often used by social scientists who examine social attitudes and behavior.

The advantages of using NORC data are:

- Identical questions have been asked each year since 1972.
- There is a large variety of questions asked about social attitudes and behavior.

The disadvantages of NORC data are:

- As with NES, the sample sizes are small relative to exit polls.
- NORC is not tied to the election cycle. Polling is usually conducted in February.
- Relatively few questions are asked about political behavior. Although respondents are asked who they voted for in the last presidential election and their party identification, respondents are not asked about voting in other elections, how often they participate in political activities, or their attitudes toward specific candidates.

Other Sources of Data

Some of the major polling organizations listed below provided free computer runs to compare the size of the gender gaps (presidential, congressional, and party identification) from one organization to another (see analysis in Chapter 3). In one situation, we paid for this service.

- Chicago Council on Foreign Relations (CCFR). We used the CCFR national survey on foreign relations conducted in 1994.
- Gallup. The Gallup organization provided data going back to 1940.[8] For the most part, these data came from Gallup's final pre-election surveys.
- *Los Angeles Times* (LAT). LAT provided results of a postelection survey in 1980 and exit polling data from presidential election years beginning in 1984.

As previously discussed, the three major networks created VRS/VNS in 1990. The following sources provided data from earlier elections:

- ABC. Exit poll data between 1982 and 1988.
- CBS. CBS and the *New York Times* joined in 1980 to conduct exit polls. The CBS data go back to 1972.
- NBC. Exit poll data between 1980 and 1988.

There are three ways to obtain data on voting behavior: (1) conducting exit polls outside designated precincts immediately after respondents vote; (2) interviewing respondents at their home by telephone or in face-to-face interviews before the election;[9] or (3) interviewing respondents at their home by telephone or in face-to-face interviews after the election.

In researching this book, we spoke to many people in the polling industry. There is general agreement that data collected before an election are the most problematic. However, people who conduct exit polls are highly cynical of the quality of election data collected from respondents at their homes after the election. These critics claim that such data are collected months after the election, respondents lie as to whether or not they voted, the election results are highly inaccurate, and the sample sizes are too small. People who conduct face-to-face interviews are equally disparaging of exit polls. They claim that exit-poll questionnaires are too short, the choice of sample precincts is too limited, the quality of some of the interviewers is suspect, and the reason VNS data are more accurate is that the data are "fudged" in the process of weighing. We are not in a position to state which type of survey is more accurate, but in response to these concerns, we compared and contrasted results whenever possible.[10] Given these problems, we must use caution not to overinterpret the data.

Notes

1. Norris (1994) offers three notes of cautions for those attempting to explain the gender gap. First, any such attempt needs to take into account long-term trends. One cannot simply look at one election. Second, one needs to be sensitive to significant diversity among groups of women—by race, education, and so on. Third, it is important to evaluate trends in U.S. public opinion in a cross-national context to look for parallel developments in other countries. In this book, we attempt to pay attention to the first two issues raised by Norris.

2. To be fair, most social scientists would be happy with estimates of political parameters that differ by only 1 or 2 percentage points. However, since these numbers are often reported (in this book as well) with the appearance of being exact (to the decimal place), it is useful to explain to those without advanced training (and to remind those with such training) that such data are subject to great uncertainty.

3. Kristi Andersen, Department of Political Science, Maxwell School, Syracuse University, Internet discussion group, February 9, 1994.

4. Some experts believe that reliance upon polling to analyze gender and politics is unfortunate. Baer (1993) argues that the narrow orthodoxy makes theorizing difficult and that the researchers are too inbred. She believes that it would be better to use in-depth interviewing and participant observation. Furthermore, she believes that women and politics research should concentrate more on recruitment and political parties.

5. Hereafter, the term VNS applies to both VRS and VNS.

6. We attempted to examine whether women are more likely to vote for women in congressional elections. Richard Seltzer combined information from the NWPC data base of 9,600 candidates with the VNS national data to identify the gender of the candidates in the VNS data.

There are problems with using VNS data on congressional elections to analyze this question. Exit polling was not conducted in all 435 congressional districts (e.g., exit polls were conducted in only 166 congressional districts in 1994). A more serious problem is that within each congressional district, the sample is not random and usually arises from only one or two precincts. The sample sizes from each congressional district vary widely (14 to 390). Our results were highly inconsistent and are not reported in this study. Similar inconsistent results occurred with NES data.

7. No survey was conducted in 1954.

8. Not all organizations conducted surveys in every year. In addition, questions about congressional preference and party identification were not asked in all years by each of the organizations. The tables in Chapter 3 indicate the years in which these questions were or were not asked.

9. For a discussion of pre-election survey methodology, see Voss, Gelman, and King (1995).

10. Some excellent research examines why surveys disagree. Turner (1984) found that the more amorphous the question area, the more likely there would be different results when the same question was asked by different survey organizations. Smith (1982) found a variety of differences in a collaborative experiment between the 1980 NES and the 1980 NORC GSS. In particular, more "don't knows" occurred with NES, probably because of differences in interviewer training. Crespi (1988) conducted a detailed analysis of 343 different pre-election polls to determine which factors (number of

callbacks, weighing of data, number of days to election, etc.) were most influential in predicting the accuracy of the poll.

Appendix 2: Success Rates

The tables in this section are provided to support specific findings discussed in Chapter 4. The original study upon which this chapter was based contained ninety separate tables of data. In an effort to keep this book of manageable size and scope, we opted to reproduce only those tables found in Chapter 4 and this section. Those who wish to see the complete tables for this chapter should contact the National Women's Political Caucus.

Table A2.1 Success Rates by Party, 1986–1994, State Legislature

	Men		Women	
Republicans				
State house				
Incumbents*	93.1%	(6,582)	94.8%	(1,649)
Open seat candidates	51.8	(3,638)	54.2	(909)
Challengers	9.5	(4,999)	10.9	(1,158)
State senate				
Incumbents	90.3	(1,552)	93.3	(238)
Open seat candidates	51.0	(1,043)	55.2	(194)
Challengers	11.4	(1,382)	12.2	(246)
Democrats				
State house				
Incumbents*	94.4%	(9,429)	92.6%	(2,232)
Open seat candidates*	54.2	(3,630)	51.0	(1,407)
Challengers	9.9	(3,558)	11.0	(1,245)
State senate				
Incumbents*	93.6	(2,265)	88.7	(417)
Open seat candidates	59.1	(1,045)	55.6	(302)
Challengers*	11.3	(926)	18.0	(317)

Note: Numbers in parentheses are the number of races in each category.
* $p < .05$

Table A2.2 Success Rates over Time, 1986–1994, State Legislature

	Men		Women	
State house				
Incumbents				
1986	94.6%	(3,446)	95.3%	(731)
1988	95.3	(3,304)	96.6	(729)
1990	93.1	(3,353)	94.0	(795)
1992	93.0	(2,858)	92.6	(745)
1994*	92.9	(3,050)	90.0	(881)
Open seat candidates				
1986	53.9%	(1,332)	51.3%	(351)
1988	51.8	(1,186)	49.4	(360)
1990	52.4	(1,358)	50.6	(425)
1992	53.6	(1,811)	55.0	(645)
1994	53.1	(1,581)	52.7	(535)
Challengers				
1986	8.8%	(1,777)	8.2%	(466)
1988	6.8	(1,749)	9.4	(458)
1990	10.8	(1,758)	11.4	(500)
1992	9.2	(1,613)	11.6	(507)
1994	12.7	(1,660)	14.0	(472)
State senate				
Incumbents				
1986	94.1%	(832)	96.2%	(106)
1988	93.3	(790)	93.3	(135)
1990	89.4	(795)	91.9	(123)
1992*	91.4	(794)	86.5	(170)
1994*	92.6	(679)	85.0	(140)
Open seat candidates				
1986	55.8%	(400)	52.9%	(68)
1988	54.4	(329)	60.0	(65)
1990	53.9	(395)	56.8	(95)
1992	54.6	(570)	59.7	(159)
1994	55.9	(438)	49.2	(126)
Challengers				
1986	8.6%	(509)	11.6%	(86)
1988	9.7	(485)	15.8	(101)
1990	14.3	(502)	17.9	(123)
1992	12.3	(472)	16.9	(142)
1994	13.6	(404)	12.4	(121)

Note: Numbers in parentheses are the number of races in each category.
$* p < .05$

Table A2.3 Success Rates by Party, 1972–1994, U.S. House

	Men		Women	
Republicans				
Incumbents	93.9%	(1,700)	98.8%	(82)
Open seat candidates	47.5	(520)	40.5	(42)
Challengers	5.8	(2,110)	3.7	(190)
Democrats				
Incumbents*	95.4%	(2,615)	90.7%	(151)
Open seat candidates	55.1	(503)	52.0	(75)
Challengers	6.6	(1,399)	4.4	(206)

Note: Numbers in parentheses are the number of races in each category.
* $p < .05$

Table A2.4 Success Rates over Time, 1972–1994, U.S. House

	Incumbents				Open Seat Candidates				Challengers			
	Men		Women		Men		Women		Men		Women	
1972	97.2%	(361)	90.0%	(10)	50.0%	(106)	66.7%	(6)	2.6%	(308)	6.3%	(16)
1974	89.0	(364)	100.0	(11)	48.5	(99)	80.0	(5)	12.9	(294)	7.7	(26)
1976	96.7	(359)	100.0	(15)	53.2	(94)	33.3	(6)	4.3	(299)	0.0	(32)
1978	95.2	(356)	85.7	(14)	52.4	(103)	50.0	(6)	6.6	(287)	0.0	(25)
1980	91.9	(370)	100.0	(14)	51.9	(79)	16.7	(6)	8.8	(307)	9.7	(31)
1982	93.0	(357)	93.8	(16)	52.5	(101)	33.3	(12)	7.4	(296)	3.8	(26)
1984	95.5	(381)	100.0	(19)	53.1	(49)	25.0	(4)	5.3	(300)	2.4	(41)
1986	98.4	(368)	100.0	(18)	50.0	(76)	60.0	(5)	1.8	(281)	2.6	(38)
1988	98.2	(379)	100.0	(22)	53.2	(47)	25.0	(4)	2.0	(297)	3.2	(31)
1990	96.0	(375)	100.0	(24)	52.1	(48)	37.5	(8)	4.6	(285)	2.7	(37)
1992	93.9	(314)	88.5	(26)	50.4	(135)	56.4	(39)	6.2	(273)	4.9	(41)
1994	92.1	(331)	81.8	(44)	50.0	(86)	50.0	(16)	11.3	(282)	5.8	(52)

Note: Numbers in parentheses are the number of races in each category.

Table A2.5 Open Seat Races, 1972–1994, U.S. House

	Percentage of Open Seat Candidates Who Were Women	Percentage of Seats Won in Open Seat Races
1972	5.4%	13.4%
1974	4.8	12.2
1976	6.0	12.2
1978	5.5	13.4
1980	7.1	9.9
1982	10.6	13.4
1984	7.5	6.3
1986	6.2	9.6
1988	7.8	6.1
1990	14.3	6.6
1992	22.4	21.1
1994	15.7	11.9

Table A2.6 Percentage of Candidates Who Were Women, by Party

	Republicans		Democrats	
State house 1986–1994	19.6%	(18,935)	22.7%	(21,501)
State senate 1986–1994	14.6	(4,655)	19.7	(5,272)
U.S. House 1972–1994	6.8	(4,644)	8.7	4,949)
U.S. Senate 1972–1994	7.7	(389)	8.1	(395)
Governor 1972–1994	5.0	(319)	8.2	(317)

Note: Numbers in parentheses are the number of candidates in each category.

Table A2.7 Success Rates by Party Without Regard to Sex

	Republicans	Democrats
State house, 1986–1994		
Incumbents	93.4%	94.0%
Open seat candidates	52.3	53.3
Challengers	9.8	10.2
State senate, 1986–1994		
Incumbents	90.7%	92.8%
Open seat candidates	51.7	58.4
Challengers	11.5	13.0
U.S. House, 1972–1994		
Incumbents	94.1%	95.2%
Open seat candidates	47.0	54.7
Challengers	5.7	6.4
U.S. Senate, 1972–1994		
Incumbents	80.8%	84.5%
Open seat candidates	55.6	45.1
Challengers	16.0	19.3
Governor, 1972–1994		
Incumbents	73.2%	81.0%
Open seat candidates	42.0	55.6
Challengers	19.0	27.1

Table A2.8 Percentage of Candidates Who Were Women, by Year

	Incumbents			Open Seats			Challengers			All Candidates		
	Women	Candidates	Percent	Women	Candidates	Percent	Women	Candidates	Percent	Women	Candidates	Percent
State House												
1986	731	4,177	17.5%	351	1,683	20.9%	466	2,243	20.8%	1,548	8,103	19.1%
1988	729	4,033	18.1%	360	1,546	23.3%	458	2,207	20.8%	1,547	7,786	19.9%
1990	795	4,148	19.2%	425	1,783	23.8%	500	2,258	22.1%	1,720	8,189	21.0%
1992	745	3,603	20.7%	645	2,456	26.3%	507	2,120	23.9%	1,897	8,179	23.2%
1994	881	3,931	22.4%	535	2,116	25.3%	472	2,132	22.1%	1,888	8,179	23.1%
Totals	3,881	19,892	19.5%	2,316	9,584	24.2%	2,403	10,960	21.9%	8,600	40,436	21.3%
State Senate												
1986	106	938	11.3%	68	468	14.5%	86	595	14.5%	260	2001	13.0%
1988	135	925	14.6%	65	394	16.5%	101	586	17.2%	301	1905	15.8%
1990	123	918	13.4%	95	490	19.4%	123	625	19.7%	341	2033	16.8%
1992	170	964	17.6%	159	729	21.8%	142	614	23.1%	471	2307	20.4%
1994	140	819	17.1%	126	564	22.3%	121	525	23.0%	387	1908	20.3%
Totals	674	4,564	14.8%	513	2,645	19.4%	573	2,945	19.5%	1,760	10,154	17.3%
U.S. House												
1972	10	371	2.7%	6	112	5.4%	16	324	4.9%	32	807	4.0%
1974	11	375	2.9%	5	104	4.8%	26	320	8.1%	42	799	5.3%
1976	15	374	4.0%	6	100	6.0%	32	331	9.7%	53	805	6.6%
1978	14	370	3.8%	6	109	5.5%	25	312	8.0%	45	791	5.7%
1980	14	384	3.6%	6	85	7.1%	31	338	9.2%	51	807	6.3%
1982	16	373	4.3%	12	113	10.6%	26	322	8.1%	54	808	6.7%
1984	19	400	4.8%	4	53	7.5%	41	341	12.0%	64	794	8.1%
1986	18	386	4.7%	5	81	6.2%	38	319	11.9%	61	786	7.8%
1988	22	401	5.5%	4	51	7.8%	31	328	9.5%	57	780	7.3%
1990	24	399	6.0%	8	56	14.3%	37	322	11.5%	69	777	8.9%
1992	26	340	7.6%	39	174	22.4%	41	314	13.1%	106	828	12.8%
1994	44	375	11.7%	16	102	15.7%	52	334	15.6%	112	811	13.8%
Totals	233	4,548	5.1%	117	1,140	10.3%	396	3,905	10.1%	746	9,593	7.8%

U.S. Senate												
1972	1	25	4.0%	0	14	0.0%	1	25	4.0%	2	64	3.1%
1974	0	24	0.0%	0	18	0.0%	3	22	13.6%	3	64	4.7%
1976	0	24	0.0%	0	16	0.0%	1	23	4.3%	1	63	1.6%
1978	0	21	0.0%	1	21	4.8%	1	21	4.8%	2	63	3.2%
1980	0	24	0.0%	2	18	11.1%	3	24	12.5%	5	66	7.6%
1982	0	30	0.0%	1	6	16.7%	2	30	6.7%	3	66	4.5%
1984	1	28	3.6%	0	8	0.0%	9	28	32.1%	10	64	15.6%
1986	1	28	3.6%	3	10	30.0%	2	28	7.1%	6	66	9.1%
1988	0	27	0.0%	1	12	8.3%	1	27	3.7%	2	66	3.0%
1990	1	31	3.2%	1	6	16.7%	6	27	22.2%	8	64	12.5%
1992	1	26	3.8%	3	16	18.8%	7	26	26.9%	11	68	16.2%
1994	2	26	7.7%	2	18	11.1%	5	26	19.2%	9	70	12.9%
Totals	7	314	2.2%	14	163	8.6%	41	307	13.4%	62	784	7.9%
Governor												
1972	0	9	0.0%	0	18	0.0%	0	9	0.0%	0	36	0.0%
1973	0	0	—	0	3	0.0%	0	0	—	0	3	0.0%
1974	0	21	0.0%	1	28	3.6%	2	21	9.5%	3	70	4.3%
1975	0	0	—	0	4	0.0%	0	0	—	0	4	0.0%
1976	0	7	0.0%	2	14	14.3%	0	7	0.0%	2	28	7.1%
1977	0	1	0.0%	0	2	0.0%	0	1	0.0%	0	4	0.0%
1978	1	21	4.8%	0	30	0.0%	0	21	0.0%	1	72	1.4%
1979	0	0	—	0	4	0.0%	0	0	—	0	4	0.0%
1980	0	10	0.0%	0	6	0.0%	0	10	0.0%	0	26	0.0%
1981	0	0	—	0	4	0.0%	0	0	—	0	4	0.0%
1982	0	24	0.0%	1	24	4.2%	1	24	4.2%	2	72	2.8%
1983	0	0	—	1	4	25.0%	0	0	—	1	4	25.0%
1984	0	6	0.0%	1	14	7.1%	0	6	0.0%	1	26	3.8%
1985	0	1	0.0%	0	2	0.0%	0	1	0.0%	0	4	0.0%
1986	1	17	5.9%	5	38	13.2%	2	16	12.5%	8	71	11.3%
1987	0	0	—	0	4	0.0%	0	0	—	0	4	0.0%
1988	1	9	11.1%	0	6	0.0%	1	9	11.1%	2	24	8.3%
1989	0	0	—	0	4	0.0%	0	0	—	0	4	0.0%
1990	1	23	4.3%	4	26	15.4%	3	23	13.0%	8	72	11.1%
1991	0	1	0.0%	0	2	0.0%	0	1	0.0%	0	4	0.0%
1992	0	4	0.0%	2	16	12.5%	1	4	25.0%	3	24	12.5%
1993	0	1	0.0%	1	2	50.0%	1	1	100.0%	2	4	50.0%
1994	1	21	4.8%	5	30	16.7%	3	21	14.3%	9	72	12.5%
Totals	5	176	2.8%	23	285	8.1%	14	175	8.0%	42	636	6.6%

Appendix 3: Gender Gap by Individual Race

Senator, 1994
Democratic Woman v. Republican Man

Gap	Democrat	Republican	State		%Dem	%Rep
11.2	Dianne Feinstein	Michael Huffington	CA	Women	52.6	37.9
				Men	41.4	52.0
11.1	Ann Wynia	Rod Grams	MN	Women	49.8	44.4
				Men	38.7	54.1

11.2 points average gender gap

Senator, 1994
Democratic Man v. Republican Man

Gap	Democrat	Republican	State		%Dem	%Rep
13.6	Bob Carr	Spencer Abraham	MI	Women	49.7	46.1
				Men	36.1	58.0
13.0	Paul Sarbanes	William Brock	MD	Women	65.8	34.2
				Men	52.8	47.2
11.9	Ron Sims	Slade Gorton	WA	Women	50.3	49.7
				Men	38.4	61.6
11.2	Frank Lautenberg	Garabed Haytaian	NJ	Women	55.7	40.8
				Men	44.5	53.1
10.4	Edward Kennedy	Mitt Romney	MA	Women	63.3	36.1
				Men	52.9	45.7
9.7	Sam Coppersmith	John Kyl	AZ	Women	44.3	49.3
				Men	34.6	57.6

Note: Percentages do not always add up to 100 because of rounding and because there were additional candidates in some races.

Senator, 1994
Democratic Man v. Republican Man (continued)

Gap	Democrat	Republican	State		%Dem	%Rep
9.6	Alan Wheat	John Ashcroft	MO	Women	40.8	55.4
				Men	31.2	64.5
9.5	Charles Robb	Oliver North	VA	Women	49.9	39.0
				Men	40.4	48.0
9.1	Joseph Lieberman	Jerry Labriola	CT	Women	71.3	26.4
				Men	62.2	36.1
8.9	Jeff Bingaman	Colin McMillan	NM	Women	58.6	41.4
				Men	49.7	50.3
8.3	Herb Kohl	Robert Welch	WI	Women	62.6	37.0
				Men	54.3	44.0
8.2	Jim Sasser	Bill Frist	TN	Women	45.7	52.2
				Men	37.5	60.5
8.2	Mike Sullivan	Craig Thomas	WY	Women	43.2	54.4
				Men	35.0	63.4
6.7	Jim Cooper	Fred Thompson	TN	Women	41.1	56.7
				Men	34.4	63.8
6.7	Richard Bryan	Hal Furman	NV	Women	54.0	35.2
				Men	47.3	47.1
6.1	Dave McCurdy	James Inhofe	OK	Women	42.6	51.4
				Men	36.5	59.7
4.9	Joel Hyatt	Mike DeWine	OH	Women	41.3	51.9
				Men	36.4	54.7
4.0	Jack Mudd	Conrad Burns	MT	Women	39.9	60.1
				Men	35.9	64.1
3.2	Harris Wofford	Rick Santorum	PA	Women	48.8	47.1
				Men	45.6	50.6
2.3	Hugh Rodham	Connie Mack	FL	Women	30.4	69.6
				Men	28.1	71.9
–0.3	Charles Oberly	William Roth	DE	Women	42.1	55.9
				Men	42.4	55.6

7.9 points average gender gap

Senator, 1994
Democratic Man v. Republican Woman

Gap	Democrat	Republican	State		%Dem	%Rep
7.6	Bob Kerrey	Jan Stoney	NE	Women	58.5	41.5
				Men	50.9	49.1

Senator, 1994
Democratic Man v. Republican Woman (continued)

Gap	Democrat	Republican	State		%Dem	%Rep
2.9	Daniel Patrick Moynihan	Bernadette Castro	NY	Women	56.6	39.6
				Men	53.7	44.1
1.2	Thomas Andrews	Olympia Snowe	ME	Women	37.3	60.0
				Men	36.1	60.5
0.1	Richard Fisher	Kay B. Hutchison	TX	Women	38.3	60.5
				Men	38.2	61.0

3.0 points average gender gap

Senator, 1992
Democratic Woman v. Republican Man

Gap	Democrat	Republican	State		%Dem	%Rep
14.3	Dianne Feinstein	John Seymour	CA	Women	63.8	33.1
				Men	49.5	45.6
13.8	Barbara Boxer	Bruce Herschensohn	CA	Women	57.1	37.0
				Men	43.3	51.4
12.1	Jean Lloyd-Jones	Charles Grassley	IA	Women	33.9	66.1
				Men	21.8	78.2
9.8	Lynn Yeakel	Arlen Specter	PA	Women	53.7	46.3
				Men	43.9	56.1
9.8	Barbara Mikulski	Alan Keyes	MD	Women	75.8	24.2
				Men	66.0	34.0
8.5	Geri Rothman-Serot	Christopher Bond	MO	Women	49.0	51.0
				Men	40.5	59.5
7.2	Carol Moseley-Braun	Richard Williamson	IL	Women	58.5	41.5
				Men	51.3	48.7
7.1	Patty Murray	Rod Chandler	WA	Women	58.5	41.5
				Men	51.4	48.6
6.0	Gloria O'Dell	Bob Dole	KS	Women	35.1	60.1
				Men	29.1	66.8
1.8	Claire Sargent	John McCain	AZ	Women	33.1	56.2
				Men	31.3	57.2

9.0 points average gender gap

Senator, 1992
Democratic Man v. Republican Man

Gap	Democrat	Republican	State		%Dem	%Rep
15.4	Les AuCoin	Bob Packwood	OR	Women	55.8	44.2
				Men	40.4	59.6

Senator, 1992
Democratic Man v. Republican Man (continued)

Gap	Democrat	Republican	State		%Dem	%Rep
9.8	Patrick Leahy	James Douglas	VT	Women	61.3	38.7
				Men	51.5	48.5
9.2	Byron Dorgan	Steve Sydness	ND	Women	63.5	36.5
				Men	54.3	45.7
9.1	Robert Abrams	Alfonse D'Amato	NY	Women	53.4	46.6
				Men	44.3	55.7
6.7	Terry Sanford	Lauch Faircloth	NC	Women	51.1	48.9
				Men	44.4	55.6
6.5	Dale Bumpers	Mike Huckabee	AR	Women	61.8	38.2
				Men	55.3	44.7
6.4	Wyche Fowler	Paul Coverdell	GA	Women	52.1	44.5
				Men	45.7	51.4
6.0	Richard Shelby	Richard Sellers	AL	Women	69.3	30.7
				Men	63.3	36.7
5.3	Ben Nighthorse Campbell	Terry Considine	CO	Women	58.4	41.6
				Men	53.1	46.9
4.2	Richard Stallings	Dirk Kempthorne	ID	Women	45.0	55.0
				Men	40.8	59.2
3.7	John Rauh	Judd Gregg	NH	Women	49.1	49.0
				Men	45.4	52.3
3.7	Steve Lewis	Don Nickles	OK	Women	41.0	57.0
				Men	37.3	60.6
3.3	Harry Reid	Demar Dahl	NV	Women	53.1	40.0
				Men	49.8	42.9
3.0	John Glenn	Mike DeWine	OH	Women	56.5	43.5
				Men	53.5	46.5
2.9	Christopher Dodd	Brook Johnson	CT	Women	62.5	37.5
				Men	59.6	40.4
2.3	Bob Graham	Bill Grant	FL	Women	67.2	32.8
				Men	64.9	35.1
1.5	Russell Feingold	Robert Kasten Jr.	WI	Women	53.7	46.3
				Men	52.2	47.8
1.3	Fritz Hollings	Tommy Hartnett	SC	Women	51.9	48.1
				Men	50.6	49.4
.7	Tony Smith	Frank Murkowski	AK	Women	35.7	56.9
				Men	35.0	55.7

Senator, 1992
Democratic Man v. Republican Man (continued)

Gap	Democrat	Republican	State		%Dem	%Rep
.3	Wendell Ford	David Williams	KY	Women	64.2	35.8
				Men	63.9	36.1
.1	Joseph Hogsett	Daniel Coats	IN	Women	41.8	58.2
				Men	41.7	58.3
–.2	Daniel K. Inouye	Rick Reed	HI	Women	60.2	25.9
				Men	60.4	31.5
–2.8	Wayne Owens	Robert Bennett	UT	Women	40.3	59.7
				Men	43.1	56.9

4.3 points average gender gap

Senator, 1992
Democratic Man v. Republican Woman

Gap	Democrat	Republican	State		%Dem	%Rep
–5.6	Tom Daschle	Charlene Haar	SD	Women	64.0	35.0
				Men	69.6	28.4

–5.6 points average gender gap

Senator, 1990
Democratic Woman v. Republican Man

Gap	Democrat	Republican	State		%Dem	%Rep
8.3	Josie Heath	Hank Brown	CO	Women	46.2	51.3
				Men	37.9	60.9
–1.3	Kathy Helling	Alan Simpson	WY	Women	35.0	64.0
				Men	36.3	62.9

3.5 points average gender gap

Senator, 1990
Democratic Man v. Republican Man

Gap	Democrat	Republican	State		%Dem	%Rep
13.6	Jay Rockefeller	John Yoder	WV	Women	74.1	24.7
				Men	60.5	39.1
10.8	Al Gore	William Hawkins	TN	Women	74.4	24.7
				Men	63.6	34.4
10.4	Harvey Gantt	Jesse Helms	NC	Women	52.6	47.3
				Men	42.2	57.4
8.1	John Kerry	Jim Rappaport	MA	Women	59.6	39.6
				Men	51.5	48.1

Senator, 1990
Democratic Man v. Republican Man (continued)

Gap	Democrat	Republican	State		%Dem	%Rep
7.2	Howell Heflin	Bill Cabaniss	AL	Women	61.2	38.8
				Men	54.0	45.7
5.1	Carl Levin	Bill Schuette	MI	Women	60.8	38.4
				Men	55.7	43.4
4.9	John Durkin	Robert Smith	NH	Women	33.8	63.2
				Men	28.9	67.1
4.8	Hugh Parmer	Phil Gramm	TX	Women	39.2	59.9
				Men	34.4	63.3
4.5	Tom Harkin	Tom Tauke	IA	Women	56.0	43.5
				Men	51.5	47.5
4.3	Harry Lonsdale	Mark Hatfield	OR	Women	48.1	51.7
				Men	43.8	55.3
4.2	Neil Rolde	William Cohen	ME	Women	39.3	60.5
				Men	35.1	64.5
4.0	David Boren	Stephen Jones	OK	Women	85.7	13.5
				Men	81.7	17.5
3.7	Jim Exon	Hal Daub	NE	Women	60.5	39.4
				Men	56.8	42.8
3.3	Harvey Sloane	Mitch McConnell	KY	Women	48.9	50.1
				Men	45.6	53.3
2.5	Max Baucus	Allen Kolstad	MT	Women	70.2	29.2
				Men	67.7	30.9
2.3	Paul Wellstone	Rudy Boschwitz	MN	Women	50.0	48.8
				Men	47.7	51.6
1.1	Robert Cunningham	Strom Thurmond	SC	Women	33.9	64.0
				Men	32.8	63.6
.7	Ron Twilegar	Larry Craig	ID	Women	37.9	61.4
				Men	37.2	62.5
–.9	Baron Hill	Daniel Coats	IN	Women	45.5	53.5
				Men	46.4	52.2
–1.2	Tom Benavides	Pete Domenici	NM	Women	22.6	76.8
				Men	23.8	75.7
–3.6	Ted Muenster	Larry Pressler	SD	Women	43.8	55.5
				Men	47.4	50.9

4.3 points average gender gap

Senator, 1990
Democratic Man v. Republican Woman

Gap	Democrat	Republican	State		%Dem	%Rep
8.0	Joseph Biden	M. Jane Brady	DE	Women	66.3	32.6
				Men	58.3	40.0
6.1	Bill Bradley	Christine Whitman	NJ	Women	53.5	45.1
				Men	47.4	50.8
3.8	Paul Simon	Lynn Martin	IL	Women	66.8	32.9
				Men	63.0	36.5
.1	Daniel Akaka	Patricia Saiki	HI	Women	53.7	44.2
				Men	53.6	45.0
–.9	Claiborne Pell	Claudine Schneider	RI	Women	60.7	38.8
				Men	61.6	37.5
–9.8	Dick Williams	Nancy Kassebaum	KS	Women	20.8	78.4
				Men	30.6	68.5

1.2 points average gender gap

Governor, 1994
Democratic Woman v. Republican Man

Gap	Democrat	Republican	State		%Dem	%Rep
10.7	Kathleen Brown	Pete Wilson	CA	Women	46.4	49.7
				Men	35.7	60.1
8.8	Ann Richards	George Bush	TX	Women	49.7	49.3
				Men	40.9	58.1
7.9	Kathy Karpan	Jim Geringer	WY	Women	43.8	55.6
				Men	35.9	62.7
5.1	Dawn Clark Netsch	Jim Edgar	IL	Women	37.1	61.1
				Men	32.0	65.7
3.8	Bonnie Campbell	Terry Branstad	IA	Women	43.5	55.6
				Men	39.7	59.2

7.3 points average gender gap

Governor, 1994
Democratic Man v. Republican Man

Gap	Democrat	Republican	State		%Dem	%Rep
14.9	Howard Wolpe	John Engler	MI	Women	46.1	53.9
				Men	31.2	68.8
14.4	Jim Slattery	Bill Graves	KS	Women	43.1	56.9
				Men	28.7	71.3

Governor, 1994
Democratic Man v. Republican Man (continued)

Gap	Democrat	Republican	State		%Dem	%Rep
14.0	Jim Tucker	Sheffield Nelson	AR	Women	66.0	34.0
				Men	52.0	48.0
11.3	Roy Romer	Bruce Benson	CO	Women	61.0	34.2
				Men	49.7	43.0
9.7	John Kitzhaber	Denny Smith	OR	Women	57.4	35.4
				Men	47.7	45.4
9.5	Larry EchoHawk	Phil Batt	ID	Women	48.4	48.1
				Men	38.9	56.6
9.2	Lawton Chiles	Jeb Bush	FL	Women	54.8	45.2
				Men	45.6	54.4
8.7	Eddie Basha	Fife Symington	AZ	Women	48.9	48.2
				Men	40.2	56.6
7.3	James Folsom	Fob James	AL	Women	52.8	47.2
				Men	45.5	54.5
6.6	John Marty	Arne Carlson	MN	Women	37.6	60.9
				Men	31.0	66.5
6.2	Mario Cuomo	George Pataki	NY	Women	48.2	45.9
				Men	42.0	52.8
6.1	Ben Nelson	Gene Spence	NE	Women	77.0	23.0
				Men	70.9	29.1
5.5	Chuck Chvala	Tommy Thompson	WI	Women	33.7	65.3
				Men	28.2	68.7
5.3	Bruce King	Gary Johnson	NM	Women	42.7	45.5
				Men	37.4	53.7
5.3	Phil Bredesen	Don Sundquist	TN	Women	47.0	51.8
				Men	41.7	57.4
4.4	Mark Singel	Tom Ridge	PA	Women	42.2	43.2
				Men	37.8	47.2
4.1	Jack Mildren	Frank Keating	OK	Women	31.1	44.7
				Men	27.0	50.6
3.2	Bill Curry	John Rowland	CT	Women	34.2	33.2
				Men	31.0	39.2
2.5	Bob Miller	Jim Gibbons	NV	Women	54.0	39.0
				Men	51.5	43.2
1.5	Mark Roosevelt	William Weld	MA	Women	28.9	70.8
				Men	27.4	70.8

Governor, 1994
Democratic Man v. Republican Man (continued)

Gap	Democrat	Republican	State		%Dem	%Rep
1.4	Robert Burch	George Voinovich	OH	Women	25.6	72.1
				Men	24.2	72.0
1.4	Zell Miller	Guy Millner	GA	Women	51.8	48.2
				Men	50.4	49.6
–.8	Nick Theodore	David Beasley	SC	Women	46.9	50.5
				Men	47.7	50.9

6.6 points average gender gap

Governor, 1994
Democratic Man v. Republican Woman

Gap	Democrat	Republican	State		%Dem	%Rep
12.8	Parris Glendening	Ellen Sauerbrey	MD	Women	56.6	43.4
				Men	43.8	56.2
5.1	Joseph Brennan	Susan Collins	ME	Women	36.5	23.2
				Men	31.4	23.5

9.0 points average gender gap

Governor, 1992
Democratic Woman v. Republican Man

Gap	Democrat	Republican	State		%Dem	%Rep
9.5	Deborah Arneson	Steve Merrill	NH	Women	44.5	52.6
				Men	35.0	59.6
3.2	Dorothy Bradley	Marc Racicot	MT	Women	50.6	49.4
				Men	47.4	52.6

6.4 points average gender gap

Governor, 1992
Democratic Man v. Republican Man

Gap	Democrat	Republican	State		%Dem	%Rep
7.9	Thomas Carper	Gary Scott	DE	Women	70.1	29.5
				Men	62.2	37.1
6.5	Mike Lowry	Ken Eikenberry	WA	Women	56.7	43.3
				Men	50.2	49.8
5.5	James Hunt Jr.	Jim Gardner	NC	Women	56.4	41.2
				Men	50.9	47.0
5.5	Howard Dean	John McClaughry	VT	Women	78.3	19.6
				Men	72.8	25.1

Governor, 1992
Democratic Man v. Republican Man (continued)

Gap	Democrat	Republican	State		%Dem	%Rep
4.0	Gaston Caperton	Cleve Benedict	WV	Women	58.4	33.0
				Men	54.4	39.4
2.3	Evan Bayh	Linley Pearson	IN	Women	63.4	36.6
				Men	61.1	38.9
.7	Nicholas Spaeth	Edward Schafer	ND	Women	41.0	59.0
				Men	40.3	59.7
.4	Mel Carnahan	William Webster	MO	Women	57.9	42.1
				Men	57.5	42.5
–.1	Stewart Hanson	Michael Leavitt	UT	Women	24.0	44.4
				Men	24.1	40.3

3.6 points average gender gap

Governor, 1992
Democratic Man v. Republican Woman

Gap	Democrat	Republican	State		%Dem	%Rep
–2.7	Bruce Sundlun	Elizabeth Leonard	RI	Women	62.5	37.5
				Men	65.2	34.8

–2.7 points average gender gap

Governor, 1990
Democratic Woman v. Republican Man

Gap	Democrat	Republican	State		%Dem	%Rep
18.2	Barbara Roberts	Dave Frohnmayer	OR	Women	56.3	29.1
				Men	38.1	47.2
12.3	Dianne Feinstein	Pete Wilson	CA	Women	53.8	42.4
				Men	41.5	54.6
12.2	Ann Richards	Clayton Williams	TX	Women	55.0	38.6
				Men	42.8	53.4
–1.6	Joan Finney	Mike Hayden	KS	Women	48.9	43.7
				Men	50.5	43.6

10.3 points average gender gap

Governor, 1990
Democratic Man v. Republican Man

Gap	Democrat	Republican	State		%Dem	%Rep
11.7	Mario Cuomo	Pierre Rinfret	NY	Women	59.3	17.6
				Men	47.6	26.2

Governor, 1990
Democratic Man v. Republican Man (continued)

Gap	Democrat	Republican	State		%Dem	%Rep
9.0	Peter Welch	Richard Snelling	VT	Women	51.1	47.1
				Men	42.1	55.7
8.1	Zell Miller	Johnny Isakson	GA	Women	56.5	41.1
				Men	48.4	48.6
7.7	Ned McWherter	Dwight Henry	TN	Women	66.1	32.5
				Men	58.4	39.1
7.0	James Blanchard	John Engler	MI	Women	51.0	48.1
				Men	44.0	54.8
7.0	Dave Walters	Bill Price	OK	Women	62.2	30.7
				Men	55.2	36.9
6.5	Thomas Loftus	Tommy Thompson	WI	Women	45.0	54.9
				Men	38.5	61.0
6.3	William Schaefer	William Shepard	MD	Women	62.1	36.4
				Men	55.8	43.8
6.3	Cecil Andrus	Roger Fairchild	ID	Women	70.8	28.7
				Men	64.5	35.1
5.6	Joseph Grandmaison	Judd Gregg	NH	Women	38.4	58.1
				Men	32.8	62.4
5.1	Bob Miller	Jim Gallaway	NV	Women	69.6	28.4
				Men	64.5	33.0
4.9	Roy Romer	John Andrews	CO	Women	66.5	32.0
				Men	61.6	36.8
4.8	Paul Hubbert	Guy Hunt	AL	Women	50.2	49.8
				Men	45.4	54.4
4.5	Bill Clinton	Sheffield Nelson	AR	Women	59.4	40.0
				Men	54.9	44.8
3.7	Terry Goodard	Fife Symington	AZ	Women	51.1	48.0
				Men	47.4	50.8
3.3	Joseph Brennan	John McKernan	ME	Women	47.1	46.7
				Men	43.8	49.4
3.2	Anthony Celebrezze	George Voinovich	OH	Women	45.9	53.9
				Men	42.7	57.3
3.0	John Waihee	Fred Hemmings	HI	Women	56.9	40.6
				Men	53.9	44.5
2.8	Bruce Morrison	John Rowland	CT	Women	21.7	35.0
				Men	18.9	40.6

Governor, 1990
Democratic Man v. Republican Man (continued)

Gap	Democrat	Republican	State		%Dem	%Rep
2.5	Theo Mitchell	Carroll Campbell	SC	Women	31.6	66.6
				Men	29.1	67.3
1.1	John Silber	William Weld	MA	Women	47.8	49.1
				Men	46.7	51.5
1.0	Bruce King	Frank Bond	NM	Women	54.6	44.5
				Men	53.6	46.2
.7	Lawton Chiles	Bob Martinez	FL	Women	56.6	43.1
				Men	55.9	43.9
–.2	Bruce Sundlun	Edward DiPrete	RI	Women	74.0	25.0
				Men	74.2	24.8
–.4	Rudy Perpich	Arne Carlson	MN	Women	48.3	49.2
				Men	48.7	48.9
–.6	Donald Avenson	Terry Branstad	IA	Women	38.0	61.7
				Men	38.6	60.7
–2.2	Neil Hartigan	Jim Edgar	IL	Women	46.6	52.3
				Men	48.8	49.7
–11.0	Bob Samuelson	George Mickelson	SD	Women	34.9	65.1
				Men	45.9	53.7

3.6 points average gender gap

Governor, 1990
Democratic Man v. Republican Woman

Gap	Democrat	Republican	State		%Dem	%Rep
–.2	Ben Nelson	Kay Orr	NE	Women	48.5	49.3
				Men	48.7	48.6
–1.8	Robert Casey	Barbara Hafer	PA	Women	66.4	33.3
				Men	68.2	31.5
–4.9	Mike Sullivan	Mary Mead	WY	Women	61.5	37.6
				Men	66.4	33.6

–2.3 points average gender gap

Appendix 4: Multivariate Analyses

Methodological Constraints

Five constraints limit the analyses:

1. Linear regression instead of logistic regression is preferred to analyze voting behavior because of its greater ease of interpretation and its familiarity to readers with a casual understanding of statistics. However, linear regression techniques assume that the variable one is trying to predict not be categorical (i.e., such as whether the respondent voted Democratic or Republican). Other researchers examining the gender gap either have inappropriately used regression techniques on a categorical variable (Miller, 1988) or have used regression analysis on a proxy variable for voter choice such as 100-point feeling thermometers (Cook and Wilcox, 1995). The analysis in this book uses more complex techniques that do not assume that the dependent variable is interval level (log-linear modeling and logistic regression). We have opted to use relatively simple language in the main text and place the relevant tables and explanations in appendices and footnotes.

2. NES did not ask all the questions of interest in the years in question. For example, in 1966 no questions are included in the NES cumulative file on government spending for the poor, U.S. intervention abroad, economic outlook, or even employment status.

3. NES does not ask some questions at all. In particular:

- Respondents are asked about family income instead of personal income. It is inappropriate for this study to combine the incomes of males and females. We therefore used education as a surrogate for class.
- NES does not question respondents about whether or not

they are religiously evangelical. Church attendance is used as an alternate measure.

4. VNS did not ask attitudinal and demographic questions that would have allowed the data to be examined with the same rigor that was used to examine NES data.

In 1994 VNS asked some questions in one version of its survey that were not asked in its other version (specifically, whether the government should do more to solve the nation's problems; the respondent's assessment of the economy; and the respondent's level of education). It is impossible to examine all three variables simultaneously. When separate logistic regressions were run in 1994, gender remained statistically significant after the limited control variables were introduced. In 1992, the question on government intervention was answered by only 16 percent of the sample. Nevertheless, gender was not statistically significant after this question was controlled for at either the presidential or congressional level. The question on government intervention was not asked at all in 1990. When controls were introduced for other variables, gender remained statistically significant.

5. Complete data from the other surveys discussed in Chapter 3 was not available. Therefore, situations in which NES and other surveys disagreed could not be analyzed. For example, CBS showed a substantial gender gap in the 1988 congressional elections and NES did not (gaps = 5 and 0.4, respectively). It would not make sense to analyze the gender gap in 1988 using NES data because NES did not show a gap.

Multivariate Tables

The typical reader would not benefit if we included all the tables on which the analysis in Chapter 6 is based. Instead we have opted to include a summary table of the log-linear modeling results and examples of the logistic regression and linear regression tables.

Log-Linear Modeling

Log-linear modeling (Knoke and Burke, 1980) was used to compare models with gender excluded and included for those years in which there was a significant or borderline significant gender gap. Basically, gender was added to a model already including another explanatory variable to see if gender significantly improved the fit of the model.

Table A4.1 Log-Linear Analysis, Presidential Elections

	Change LR	Change DF	*p*-value
1992			
Gov't. guarantee jobs	3.10	1	ns
Economy last year	1.14	1	ns
1988			
Gov't. guarantee jobs	4.48	1	.03
Economy last year	0.38	1	ns
1984			
Gov't. guarantee jobs	5.49	1	.03
Economy last year	0.06	1	ns
1980			
Gov't. guarantee jobs	4.45	1	.03
Economy last year	4.81	1	.03
Gov't. guarantee jobs & Economy last year	5.23	1	.02
1972			
Gov't. guarantee jobs	2.14	1	ns
1960			
Occupation	0.69	1	ns
Age	4.22	1	.03
Marital status	2.60	1	ns, .11
1956			
Gov't. guarantee jobs	4.76	1	.03
Occupation	0.02	1	ns

Note: "ns" denotes not significant

For example, the first model in the presidential elections table (see Table A4.1) for 1992 compares two different models: (1) predicting presidential vote by whether the respondent believes that "the government in Washington should see to it that every person has a job and a good standard of living"; and (2) predicting presidential vote by the respondent's belief in the statement above and by gender.

The analysis indicates whether the second model is significantly better than the first model. In this example, the change in the likelihood chi-square ratios and degrees of freedom were 3.10 and 1, respectively. This is not statistically significant. Therefore, gender does not significantly improve a model that already contains the variable on government guaranteeing jobs and a good standard of living. In other words, the gender gap in 1992 is related to gender differences on attitudes toward government intervention to help poor Americans.

Table A4.2 Log-Linear Analysis, Congressional Elections

	Change LR	Change DF	*p*-value
1994			
Gov't. guarantee jobs	2.65	1	ns
Economy last year	5.29	1	.02
1992			
Gov't. guarantee jobs	1.72	1	ns
Economy last year	0.73	1	ns
1990			
Gov't. guarantee jobs	8.22	1	.005
Economy last year	5.66	1	.02
Gov't. guarantee jobs & Economy last year	4.50	1	.03
Marital status	3.90	1	.06
Gov't. guarantee job & Marital status	4.56	1	.03
Economy last year & Marital status	3.70	1	ns, .07
1986			
Gov't. guarantee jobs	0.19	1	ns
Economy last year	0.01	1	ns
1984			
Gov't. guarantee jobs	0.31	1	ns
Economy last year	0.30	1	ns
1982			
Gov't. guarantee jobs	1.64	1	ns
Economy last year	0.98	1	ns
1966			
Education	5.41	1	.02
1956			
Gov't. guarantee jobs	5.98	1	.02
Occupation	0.13	1	ns

Note: "ns" denotes not significant

Logistic Regression

Logistic regression enables a variant of regression analysis to be used with dichotomous dependent variables (Menard, 1995). By transforming the dependent variable (the natural logarithm of the odds [called the logit]), heteroscedacity is no longer a problem. However, the interpretation of the coefficients is more difficult than with ordinary least squares.

- The B indicates the change in the log odds with a one-unit increase in the independent variable. Using race and the 1992 presidential election as an example, black respondents have an increase of 1.67 in the logit over other respondents.
- The *p*-values (based upon the Wald statistic) reveal whether the variable (or the categories of categorical variables) are statis-

tically significant. Only statistically significant coefficients are reported.

• The Partial Rs correlate between the independent variable and the dependent variable, while the other variables are held constant.

• Odds ratios are the factors by which the odds change when the independent variable increases by one unit. In the example presented in the first entry above, blacks have a 50.36 percent increase in the odds of voting Democratic compared with other respondents.

Table A4.3 Example, Logistic Regression Analyses, Third Party Candidates Excluded, 1992 Presidential Election

	B	*p*-Value	Partial R	Odds Ratio
Gender	ns			
Education	–.16	.001	–.07	.85
Race-black	2.49	.0001	.17	12.08
Church attendance	–.61	.0001	–.10	.54
Marital status			.09	
Married	–.37	.001	–.08	.69
Never married	.71	.0002	.08	2.03
Divorced	ns			
Widowed	ns			
Age			.06	
18–29	–.36	.04	–.04	.70
30–39	–.29	.03	–.04	.75
40–49	.40	.007	.06	1.49
50–59	ns			
60+	ns			
Occupation	ns			
Prof/manag				
Sales/clerical				
Blue-collar				
Homemaker				
Not working				
Gov't. guarantee jobs	1.01	.0001	.14	2.75
U.S. stay home	.62	.0005	.08	1.86
Women-men equal role	–.25	.0001	–.13	.78
Economy last yr	.55	.0001	.20	1.73
Family finan last yr	.30	.001	.07	1.34
Constant	1.49	.0003		

Final sample size = 1,238
Lambda = .36

Notes: "ns" = not significant ($p > .10$)

Table A4.4 Least Squares Regression, Party Identification (1 = Democrat, 7 = Republican), 1994

	B	Beta	*p*-value
Race (black = 1)	–1.48	–.21	.0001
Guarantee job (yes = 1)	–.72	–.16	.0001
Education	.20	.14	.0001
Economy's performance	.41	.16	.0001
Female	.38	.09	.0001
Married	.33	.07	.002
Women equal role	.09	.07	.003
Age 60+	–.38	–.07	.003
Age 49–59	–.35	–.06	.006
U.S. stay home (yes = 1)	–.29	–.06	.01
Constant	1.36		.0001

$R^2 = .15$

Note: Not significant variables: age 29–39, age 39–49, occupation (dummies for professional, blue-collar, and homemaker), never married, church attendance, and personal financial assessment.

Appendix 5: Previous Research on Women Candidates

This book is likely to be used in undergraduate and graduate courses. Students who take these courses may want to know about other research that examines how female and male candidates differ in their success rates and why women are underrepresented as candidates. This appendix gives a brief overview of some of this previous research.

Most academic studies have found that women are as likely as men to win elections (Burrell, 1992, 1994; Darcy and Schramm, 1977; Welch, Ambrosius, Clark, and Darcy, 1985; Darcy, Welch, and Clark, 1994; and Gaddie and Bullock, 1995). The conclusions of our study do not differ substantially from the conclusions of these studies. What is different is the scope.

Many analysts view the year 1992 as pivotal since women picked up quite a few seats in the U.S. House. A number of analysts (Burrell, 1994; Carroll, 1995; Wilcox, 1994; Cook and Wilcox, 1995; Chaney and Sinclair, 1994; and Gaddie and Bullock, 1995) believe that a record number of women ran for and won U.S. House seats because of the unusually large number of open seats in the House. Wilcox (1994) also notes that much of the election hung on issues such as education and health care—issues on which women are perceived as more competent than men. Biersack and Herrnson (1994) point out that in 1992, officials from both political parties were more supportive of women candidates. Most of these analysts also note that women were extremely successful in raising money in 1992, particularly via EMILY's List and other political action committees.

Research has also been conducted on how voters view women candidates. A variety of surveys have shown that women political candidates were perceived by respondents as having certain strengths relative to men, and men were perceived as having other strengths relative to women. In general, women candidates were perceived favorably on health care, education, and meeting the needs of the middle class; men were perceived more favorably in areas of foreign affairs, defense, and crime, as well as having more expertise in general.[1]

Some studies of likely voters gave subjects different names (male and female) for the same hypothetical candidates to see how a candidate's gender might influence attitudes. Sapiro (1981–1982) and Leeper (1991) found that women candidates can be aggressive and send tough messages and that voters perceive women as being stronger in some areas (e.g., education) than men. Ekstrand and Eckert (1981) found no such differences. These studies are problematic in that they rely upon undergraduate students and very short candidate profiles.

Three types of structural issues affect the process of women becoming candidates and winning elections, according to some researchers: (1) Incumbency places roadblocks for women running for office (see, for example, Carroll, 1995:158–162; and Darcy, Welch, and Clark, 1994:Ch. 6); (2) women are more likely to run in multimember districts than in single-member districts (Rule, 1990; Matland and Brown, 1992; Darcy, Welch, and Clark, 1994); and (3) women are underrepresented in management and the professions (Welch, 1978; and Darcy, Welch, and Clark, 1994).

Other researchers believe that women are less likely to run for public office because they have less political ambition than men (Costantini, 1977, 1990; Fowlkes, Perkins, and Rinehart, 1979; Clark, Hadley, and Darcy, 1989; Sapiro, 1984). It is believed that women appear to have less ambition because men and women differently evaluate other priorities (children and family). However, some researchers believe that the ambition gap between men and women appears to be narrowing as women are currently more likely to be employed outside the household and to want to affect political change.

Little research has been done on the relationship between women candidates and women voters. Zipp and Plutzer (1985, 1996) analyzed statewide races in 1982 and 1992. For the most part, they found that voters tended to ignore the gender of the candidate. The work of Zipp and Plutzer was pioneering. Unfortunately, they made no comparisons to races in which men ran against men.

A 1992 study (*Public Perspective*, 1992) examined thirty-five statewide races from 1980 to 1990 in which a woman ran. The author concluded that "women have not voted for women in significantly greater numbers than men have," defining "significant" as a difference of 10 percentage points or more. This study did not compare the gender gap among women candidates with the gender gap among men candidates, nor did it take into account the effect of party on the gender gap. A rebuttal to this study written later in 1992 countered that the data in fact demonstrated that women do vote for women if the woman candidate is a Democrat (Smith and Selfa, 1992). Again, only races involving women were examined, and the gender gaps were not compared with those in men's races.

Cook and Wilcox (1995) used VNS data to study 1990 and 1992 races for the U.S. Senate. They found that after controlling for partisanship, the gender gap (the percentage of women voting Democratic minus the percentage of men voting Democratic) was greatest in six races featuring Democratic women candidates who ran credible races.

Cook (1994) used data from NES and VRS to analyze U.S. Senate elections from 1988 to 1992. She found that partisanship was more important than the candidate's gender in 1990, but highly qualified Republican women attracted more female voters than did Republican men. In 1992 the average gender gap when Democratic women were on the ballot was more than double the gap found in all-male contests, and it was negative in the one race in which a Republican woman ran.

Note

1. See (1) a 1972 study of 4,020 conducted by Louis Harris (Sapiro, 1984); (2) a 1983 study of 200 registered voters conducted by Yankelovich, Skelly, and White for the National Women's Political Caucus (1984); (3) a 1987 survey of 1,502 registered voters conducted by Hickman-Maslin Research for the National Women's Political Caucus (1987); and (4) a 1991 survey conducted for EMILY's List, National Women's Political Caucus, and Women's Campaign Fund of 1,160 registered voters.

References

Abramowitz, Alan I. (1995). "It's Abortion, Stupid: Policy Voting in the 1992 Presidential Election." *Journal of Politics*, 57:176–186.

Abzug, Bella S. (1984). *Gender Gap: Bella Abzug's Guide to Political Power for American Women*. Boston: Houghton Mifflin.

Almquist, Elizabeth (1991). "Labor Market Gender Inequality in Minority Groups," in Judith Lorber and Susan A. Farrell (eds.), *The Social Construction of Gender*. Newbury Park, Calif.: Sage Publications. Ch. 9, 180–192.

Amato, Paul R., and Alan Booth (1995). "Changes in Gender Role Attitudes and Perceived Marital Quality." *American Sociological Review*, 60:58–66.

Baer, Denise L. (1993). "Political Parties: The Missing Variable in Women and Politics Research." *Political Research Quarterly*, 46:547–576.

Baxter, Sandra, and Marjorie Lansing (1983). *Women and Politics: The Visible Majority*. Ann Arbor: University of Michigan Press.

Bendyna, Mary E., and Celinda C. Lake (1994). "Gender and Voting in the 1992 Presidential Election," in Elizabeth Adell Cook, Sue Thomas, and Clyde Wilcox (eds.), *The Year of the Woman: Myths and Reality*. Boulder, Colo.: Westview Press.

Bennett, Linda L. M. (1986). "The Gender Gap: When an Opinion Gap Is Not a Voting Bloc." *Social Science Quarterly*, 67:613–625.

Bernstein, Jared. (1995). *Where's the Payoff? The Gap Between Black Academic Progress and Economic Gains*. Washington, D.C.: Economic Policy Institute.

Bernstein, Robert A. (1986). "Why Are There So Few Women in the House?" *Western Political Quarterly*, 39:155–164.

Beutel, Ann M., and Margaret Mooney Marini (1995). "Gender and Values." *American Sociological Review*, 60:436–448.

Biersack, Robert, and Paul S. Herrnson (1994). "Political Parties and the Year of the Woman," in Elizabeth Adell Cook, Sue Thomas, and Clyde Wilcox (eds.), *The Year of the Woman: Myths and Reality*. Boulder, Colo.: Westview Press. Ch. 9, 161–180.

Blau, Francine D., and Lawrence M. Kahn (1994). "Rising Wage Inequality and the U.S. Gender Gap." *American Economic Review*, 84: 23–28.

Bolce, Louis (1985). "The Role of Gender in Recent Presidential Elections: Reagan and the Reverse Gender Gap." *Presidential Studies Quarterly*, 15:372–385.

Bonk, Kathy (1988). "The Selling of the 'Gender Gap': The Role of Organized Feminism," in Carol M. Mueller (ed.), *The Politics of the Gender Gap: The Social Construction of Political Influence.* Newbury Park, Calif.: Sage Publications. Ch. 4, 82–101.

Borger, Gloria (1995). "What Do Women Want?" *U.S. News & World Report,* August 14, p. 27.

Burrell, Barbara C. (1994). *A Woman's Place Is in the House: Campaigning for Congress in the Feminist Era.* Ann Arbor: University of Michigan Press.

——— (1992). "Women Candidates in Open-Seat Primaries for the U.S. House: 1968–1990." *Legislative Studies Quarterly,* 17:493–508.

Campbell, Angus, Philip E. Converse, Warren E. Miller, and Donald E. Stokes (1960). *The American Voter.* New York: John Wiley.

Carroll, Susan J. (1988). "Women's Autonomy and the Gender Gap: 1980 and 1982," in Carol M. Mueller (ed.), *The Politics of the Gender Gap: The Social Construction of Political Influence.* Newbury Park, Calif.: Sage Publications. Ch. 11, 236–257.

——— (1995). *Women as Candidates in American Politics.* Bloomington: Indiana University Press.

Cavanagh, Thomas E. (1981). "Changes in American Voter Turnout, 1964–1976." *Political Science Quarterly,* 96: 53–65.

Center for the American Woman and Politics (1996). "Women in Elective Office 1996," fact sheet.

Chaney, Carole, and Barbara Sinclair (1994). "Women and the 1992 House Elections," in Elizabeth Adell Cook, Sue Thomas, and Clyde Wilcox (eds.), *The Year of the Woman: Myths and Reality.* Boulder, Colo.: Westview Press. Ch. 7, 123–139.

Clark, Janet, Charles D. Hadley, and R. Darcy (1989). "Political Ambition Among Men and Women State Party Leaders: Testing the Countersocialization Perspective." *American Politics Quarterly,* 17:194–207.

Conover, Pamela Johnston (1988). "Feminists and the Gender Gap." *Journal of Politics,* 50:985–1010.

Cook, Elizabeth Adell (1994). "Voter Response to Women Senate Candidates," in Elizabeth Adell Cook, Sue Thomas, and Clyde Wilcox (eds.), *The Year of the Woman: Myths and Reality.* Boulder, Colo.: Westview Press. Ch. 12, 217–236.

Cook, Elizabeth Adell, and Clyde Wilcox (1991). "Feminism and the Gender Gap—A Second Look." *The Journal of Politics,* 53:1111–1122.

——— (1995). "Women Voters in the Year of the Woman," in Herbert Weisberg (ed.), *Democracy's Feast: Elections in America.* Chatham, N.J.: Chatham House. 195–219.

Cook, Elizabeth Adell, Ted G. Jelen, and Clyde Wilcox (1992). *Between Two Absolutes: Public Opinion and the Politics of Abortion.* Boulder, Colo.: Westview Press.

Costantini, Edmond (1977). "Women as Politicians: The Social Background, Personality and Political Careers of Female Party Leaders," in Marianne Githens and Jewel L. Prestage (eds.), *A Portrait of Marginality: The Political Behavior of the American Woman.* New York: David McKay Company. Ch. 13, 221–240.

——— (1990). "Political Women and Political Ambition: Closing the Gender Gap." *American Journal of Political Science,* 34:740–770.

Cott, Nancy F. (1995). "Across the Great Divide: Women in Politics Before and After 1920," in Marjorie Spruill Wheeler (ed.), *One Woman, One Vote: Rediscovering the Woman Suffrage Movement.* Troutdale, Ore.: New Sage Press. Ch. 19, 353–372.

Cotter, David A., et al. (1995). "Occupational Gender Segregation and the Earnings Gap: Changes in the 1980s." *Social Science Research,* 24:439–454.

Crespi, Irving (1988). *Pre-Election Polling: Sources of Accuracy and Error.* New York: Russell Sage Foundation.

Darcy, R., and James R. Choike (1986). "A Formal Analysis of Legislative Turnover: Women Candidates and Legislative Representation." *American Journal of Political Science,* 30:247–253.

Darcy, R., and Sarah Slavin Schramm (1977). "When Women Run Against Men." *Public Opinion Quarterly,* 41:1–12.

Darcy, R., Susan Welch, and Janet Clark (1994). *Women, Elections and Representation.* Lincoln: University of Nebraska Press.

Davis, James Allan, and Tom W. Smith (1994). *General Social Surveys, 1972–1994* [Computer File]. Chicago: National Opinion Research Center [Producer]; and Storrs, Conn.: The Roper Center for Public Opinion Research, University of Connecticut [Distributor].

———. (1992). *The NORC General Social Survey: A User's Guide.* Newbury Park, Calif.: Sage Publications.

Deitch, Cynthia (1988). "Sex Differences in Support for Government Spending," in Carol M. Mueller (ed.), *The Politics of the Gender Gap: The Social Construction of Political Influence.* Newbury Park, Calif.: Sage Publications. Ch. 9, 192–216.

Edsall, Thomas B. (1995). "Pollsters View Gender Gap as Political Fixture." *Washington Post,* August 15, p. 1.

Ekstrand, Laurie E., and William A. Eckert (1981). "The Impact of Candidate's Sex on Voter Choice." *Western Political Quarterly,* 34:78–87.

EMILY's List (1989). *Campaigning in a Different Voice.* Spring.

EMILY's List, National Women's Political Caucus, and Women's Campaign Fund (1991). *Winning with Women.* A survey funded by Philip Morris Companies.

England, Paula, and Lori McCreary (1987). "Gender Inequality in Paid Employment," in Beth B. Hess and Myra Marx Ferree (eds.), *Analyzing Gender: A Handbook of Social Science Research.* Newbury Park, Calif.: Sage Publications. Ch. 11, 286–320.

Erikson, Robert S., Norman R. Luttbeg, and Kent L. Tedin (1992). "Ideology as Liberalism-Conservatism: Are Americans Ideologues?" in *American Public Opinion.* 4th edition. New York: Macmillan. Ch. 4.1, 79–105.

Ferree, Myra Marx (1987). "She Works Hard for a Living: Gender and Class on the Job," in Beth B. Hess and Myra Marx Ferree (eds.), *Analyzing Gender: A Handbook of Social Science Research.* Newbury Park, Calif.: Sage Publications. Ch. 12, 322–347.

Firebaugh, Glenn, and Kevin Chen (1995). "Vote Turnout of Nineteenth Century Women: The Enduring Effect of Disenchantment." *American Journal of Sociology,* 100:972–996.

Flexner, Eleanor (1975). *Century of Struggle: The Woman's Rights Movement in the United States.* Cambridge: Harvard University Press.

Fowlkes, Diane L., Jerry Perkins, and Sue Tolleson Rinehart (1979). "Gender Roles and Party Roles." *American Political Science Review,* 73:772–780.

Frankovic, Kathleen A. (1988). "The Ferraro Factor: The Women's Movement, The Polls, and the Press," in Carol M. Mueller (ed.), *The*

Politics of the Gender Gap: The Social Construction of Political Influence. Newbury Park, Calif.: Sage Publications. Ch. 5, 102–123.

Furnham, Adrian, and Richard Rawles (1995). "Sex Differences in the Estimation of Intelligence." *Journal of Social Behavior and Personality,* 10:741–748.

Gaddie, Ronald Keith, and Charles S. Bullock III (1995). "Congressional Elections and the Year of the Woman: Structural and Elite Influences on Female Candidacies." *Social Science Quarterly,* 76:749–762.

Gans, Curtis (1995). "Final Report on 1994 Mid-Term Election." Committee for the Study of the American Electorate.

Gilens, Martin (1988). "Gender and Support for Reagan: A Comprehensive Model of Presidential Approval." *American Journal of Political Science,* 32:19–49.

Goldin, Claudia (1990). *Understanding the Gender Gap: An Economic History of American Women.* New York: Oxford University Press.

Gray, John (1992). *Men Are from Mars: Women Are from Venus: A Practical Guide for Improving Communication and Getting What You Want in Your Relationship.* New York: HarperCollins.

Gurin, Patricia (1985). "Women's Gender Consciousness." *Public Opinion Quarterly,* 49:143–163.

Harwood, John (1995). "'Sluggish Revolution' Has Voters Thinking Politicians Are All Alike." *Wall Street Journal,* August 28, p. A1.

Henry, Sherrye (1994). *The Deep Divide.* New York: Macmillan.

Hill, Kim Quaile, and Patricia A. Hurley (1984). "Nonvoters in Voters' Clothing: The Impact of Voting Behavior Misreporting on Voting Behavior Research." *Social Science Quarterly,* 65:219–226.

Jackman, M. R. (1981). "Education and Policy Commitment to Racial Integration." *American Journal of Political Science,* 22:256–269.

Jones, Kathleen B. (1985). "Toward the Revision of Politics," in Kathleen B. Jones and Anna G. Jónasdóttir (eds.), *The Political Interests of Gender: Developing Theory and Research with a Feminist Face.* Newbury Park, Calif.: Sage Publications. Ch. 2, 11–32.

Kahn, Kim Fridkin, and Edie N. Goldenberg (1991). "Women Candidates in the News: An Examination of Gender Differences in U.S. Senate Campaign Coverage." *Public Opinion Quarterly,* 55:180–199.

Katosh, John, and Michael Traugott (1981). "The Consequence of Validated and Self-Reported Voting Measures." *Public Opinion Quarterly,* 45:519–535.

Kenski, Henry C. (1988). "The Gender Factor in a Changing Electorate," in Carol M. Mueller (ed.), *The Politics of the Gender Gap: The Social Construction of Political Influence.* Newbury Park, Calif.: Sage Publications. Ch. 2, 38–60.

Knoke, David, and Peter J. Burke (1980). *Loglinear Models.* Newbury Park, Calif.: Sage Publications.

Lacayo, Richard (1995). "America's Mood Swings." *Time Magazine,* November 20, p. 66ff.

Ladd, Everett Carl (1996). "A Gap, Not a Chasm." *Weekly Standard,* February 19.

Lansing, Marjorie (1974). "The American Woman: Voter and Activist," in Jane S. Jacquette, *Women in Politics.* New York: John Wiley & Sons.

Leeper, Mark Stephen (1991). "The Impact of Prejudice on Female Candidates: An Experimental Look at Voter Inference." *American Political Quarterly,* 19: 248–261.

Maguire, Kathleen, and Ann L. Pastore (eds.) (1994). *Sourcebook of Criminal Justice Statistics.* U.S. Department of Justice, Bureau of Justice Statistics. Washington, D.C.: GPO.

Mansbridge, Jane J. (1985). "Myth and Reality: The ERA and the Gender Gap in the 1980 Election." *Public Opinion Quarterly,* 49:164–178.

Matland, Richard E., and Deborah Dwight Brown (1992). "District Magnitude's Effect on Female Representation in U.S. State Legislatures." *Legislative Studies Quarterly,* 17:469–492.

Menard, Scott (1995). *Applied Logistic Regression Analysis.* Thousand Oaks, Calif.: Sage Publications.

Miller, Arthur (1988). "Gender and the Vote: 1988," in Carol M. Mueller (ed.), *The Politics of the Gender Gap: The Social Construction of Political Influence.* Newbury Park, Calif.: Sage Publications. Ch. 12, 258–282.

Miller, Arthur, Anne Hildreth, and Grace L. Simmons (1985). "The Mobilization of Gender Group Consciousness," in Kathleen B. Jones and Anna G. Jónasdóttir (eds.), *The Political Interests of Gender: Developing Theory and Research with a Feminist Face.* Newbury Park, Calif.: Sage Publications. Ch. 6, 106–134.

Miller, Warren E. (1994). *American National Election Studies Cumulative Data File, 1952–1992* [Computer File]. 7th release. Ann Arbor: University of Michigan, Center for Political Studies [Producer] and Inter-University Consortium for Political and Social Research [Distributor].

Mishel, Lawrence, and Jared Bernstein (1994). *The State of Working America: 1994–95.* New York: M. E. Sharpe.

Mueller, Carol M. (1988). "The Empowerment of Women: Polling and the Women's Voting Bloc," in Carol M. Mueller (ed.), *The Politics of the Gender Gap: The Social Construction of Political Influence.* Newbury Park, Calif.: Sage Publications, Ch. 1, 16–36.

National Women's Political Caucus (1984). "Sex Stereotypes and Candidacy for High Level Political Office." February.

——— (1987). "The New Political Woman Survey." August.

Newman, Jody (1984). "Perception and Reality: A Study of Women Candidates and Fund-Raising." A report for the Women's Campaign Research Fund.

——— (1994). "Perception and Reality: A Study Comparing the Success of Men and Women Candidates." A report for the National Women's Political Caucus.

——— (1994). "Perception and Reality: Chapter II: A Study Comparing the Success of Men and Women in the 1994 Primaries." A report for the National Women's Political Caucus.

——— (1995). "Do Women Vote for Women?" A report for the National Women's Political Caucus.

Nie, Norman H., Sidney Verba, and John R. Petrocik (1976). *The Changing American Voter.* Cambridge: Harvard University Press.

Norris, Pippa (1994). "Gender-Related Influences on Voting Behaviour and Public Opinion." Paper presented at Research on Women and American Politics: Agenda Setting for the 21st Century Conference. Center for American Women and Politics. April 23.

Page, Benjamin I., and Robert Y. Shapiro (1992). *The Rational Public: Fifty Years of Trends in Americans' Policy Preferences.* Chicago: University of Chicago Press.

Paget, Karen M. (1993). "The Gender Gap Mystique." *The American Prospect,* 15:93–101.

Public Perspective/The American Enterprise (1992). "Do Women Vote for Women?" July/August, p. 98.
Ragsdale, Lyn, and Jerrold G. Rusk (1993). "Who Are Nonvoters: Profile from the 1990 Senate Elections." *American Journal of Political Science,* 37:721–746.
Rapoport, Ronald B., Walter J. Stone, and Alan I. Abramowitz (1990). "Sex and the Caucus Participant: The Gender Gap and Presidential Nominations." *American Journal of Political Science,* 34:725–740.
Reskin, Barbara F. (1991). "Bringing the Men Back In: Sex Differentiation and the Devaluation of Women's Work," in Judith Lorber and Susan A. Farrell (eds.), *The Social Construction of Gender.* Newbury Park, Calif.: Sage Publications. Ch. 7, 141–161.
Rule, Wilma (1990). "Why More Women Are State Legislators: A Research Note." *Western Political Quarterly,* 43:437–448.
Sapiro, Virginia (1981–1982). "If Senator Baker Were a Woman: An Experimental Study of Candidate Images." *Political Psychology,* 3: 248–261.
——— (1982). "Private Costs of Public Commitments or Public Costs of Private Commitments? Family Roles Versus Political Ambition." *American Journal of Political Studies,* 26:265–279.
——— (1984). *The Political Integration of Women: Roles Socialization, and Politics.* Urbana: University of Illinois Press.
Sapiro, Virginia, and Pamela Johnston Conover (1993). "Gender in the 1992 Electorate." Paper presented at the Annual Meeting of the American Political Science Association, Washington, D.C.
Sapiro, Virginia, and Barbara G. Farah (1980). "New Pride and Old Prejudice: Political Ambition and Role Orientations Among Female Partisan Elites." *Women and Politics,* 1:13–36.
Schlozman, Kay Lehman, Nancy Burns, and Sidney Verba (1994). "Gender and the Pathways to Participation: The Role of Resources." *The Journal of Politics,* 56:963–990.
Schlozman, Kay Lehman, Nancy Burns, Sidney Verba, and Jesse Donahue (1995). "Gender and Political Participation: Is There a Different Voice?" *American Journal of Politics,* 39:267–293.
Seib, Gerald F. (1996). "In Historic Numbers, Men and Women Split Over Presidential Race." *Wall Street Journal,* January 11, p. 1.
Shaffer, Stephen D. (1981). "A Multivariate Explanation of Decreasing Turnout in Presidential Elections, 1960–1976." *American Journal of Political Science,* 25:68–95.
Shapiro, Robert Y., and Harpreet Mahajan (1986). "Gender Differences in Policy Preferences: A Summary of Trends from the 1960s to the 1980s." *Public Opinion Quarterly,* 50:42–61.
Simon, Rita J., and Jean M. Landis (1989). "Women's and Men's Attitudes About a Woman's Place and Role." *Public Opinion Quarterly,* 53:265–276.
Smeal, Eleanor (1984). *Why and How Women Will Elect the Next President.* New York: Harper & Row.
Smith, Tom W. (1982). "House Effects and the Reproducibility of Survey Measurements: A Comparison of the 1980 GSS and the 1980 American National Election Study." *Public Opinion Quarterly,* 46:54–68.
Smith, Tom W., and Lance A. Selfa (1992). "When Do Women Vote for Women?" *The Public Perspective,* September/October, pp. 30–31.
Soule, John W., and Wilma E. McGrath (1977). "A Comparative Study of

Male-Female Political Attitudes at Citizen and Elite Levels," in Marianne Githens & Jewel L. Prestage (eds.), *A Portrait of Marginality: The Political Behavior of the American Woman.* New York: David McKay Company. Ch. 10, 178–195.

Stoper, Emily (1989). "The Gender Gap Concealed and Revealed: 1936–1984." *Journal of Political Science,* 17: 50–62.

Thomas, Sue (1994). "Women in State Legislatures: One Step at a Time," in Elizabeth Adell Cook, Sue Thomas, and Clyde Wilcox (eds.), *The Year of the Woman: Myths and Reality.* Boulder, Colo.: Westview Press. Ch. 8, 141–159.

Turner, Charles F. (1984). "Why Do Surveys Disagree? Some Preliminary Hypotheses and Some Disagreeable Examples," in Charles F. Turner and Elizabeth Martin (eds.), *Surveying Subjective Phenomenon, Vol. 2.* New York: Russell Sage Foundation. Ch. 7, 159–214.

Verba, Sidney, Norman H. Nie, and Jae-on Kim (1978). *Participation and Political Equality: A Seven Nation Comparison.* Cambridge: Cambridge University Press.

Voss, D. Stephen, Andrew Gelman, and Gary King (1995). "Preelection Survey Methodology: Details from Eight Polling Organizations, 1988 and 1992." *Public Opinion Quarterly,* 59:98–132.

Walzer, Susan (1994). "The Role of Gender in Determining Abortion Attitudes." *Social Science Quarterly,* 75:687–693.

Welch, Susan (1978). "Recruitment of Women to Public Office: A Discriminant Analysis." *Western Political Quarterly,* 17:372–380.

Welch, Susan, and Lee Sigelman (1989). "A Black Gender Gap?" *Social Science Quarterly,* 70:120 133.

Welch, Susan, and Donley T. Studlar (1990). "Multi-Member Districts and the Representation of Women: Evidence from Britain and the United States." *Journal of Politics,* 52:391–412.

Welch, Susan, Margery M. Ambrosius, Janet Clark, and Robert Darcy (1985). "The Effect of Candidate Gender on Electoral Outcomes in State Legislative Races." *Western Political Quarterly,* 38:464–475.

Welch, Susan, and Philip Secret (1989). "Sex, Race and Political Participation." *Western Political Quarterly,* 9:5–16.

Wilcox, Clyde (1991). "The Causes and Consequences of Feminist Consciousness Among Western European Women." *Comparative Political Studies,* 23:519–545.

——— (1994). "Why Was 1992 the 'Year of the Woman'? Explaining Women's Gains in 1992," in Elizabeth Adell Cook, Sue Thomas, and Clyde Wilcox (eds.), *The Year of the Woman: Myths and Reality.* Boulder, Colo.: Westview Press.

Wilcox, Clyde, Clifford W. Brown Jr., and Lynda W. Powell (1993). "Sex and the Political Contributor: The Gender Gap Among Contributors to Presidential Candidates in 1988." *Political Research Quarterly,* 46:355–369.

Williams, Christine B. (1990). "Women, Law and Politics: Recruitment Patterns in the Fifty States." *Women and Politics,* 10:103–123.

Wirls, Daniel (1986). "Reinterpreting the Gender Gap." *Public Opinion Quarterly,* 50:316–330.

Witt, Linda, Karen M. Paget, and Glenna Matthews (1995). *Running as a Woman: Gender and Power in American Politics.* New York: Free Press.

Zipp, John F., and Eric Plutzer (1985). "Gender Differences in Voting for

Female Candidates: Evidence from the 1982 Election." *Public Opinion Quarterly*, 49:179–197.
——— (1996). "Identity Politics, Partisanship, and Voting for Women Candidates." *Public Opinion Quarterly*, 60:30–57.

Index

About the Book

Though women constitute 52 percent of U.S. voters, as of October 1996 only 10 percent of the members of Congress and one of the 50 state governors are women. Why, more than 75 years after they won the right to vote, are women so severely underrepresented in elected office? Why does it seem that, as voters, their influence is not equal to their numbers?

Much of the conventional wisdom and commentary about women in the electoral system is based on impression or personal experience. This book, in contrast, presents original research and the most comprehensive analysis to date on women as candidates and voters in U.S. politics. Drawing on a massive data base on women and men as congressional candidates, as well as data from the Census Bureau, exit polls, and national election surveys, *Sex as a Political Variable* examines a number of important questions, including: Why aren't there more women in office? Is it tougher for women to win elections? What are the differences between women and men as voters with regard to party loyalty, policy issues, and the sex of a particular candidate? Supported by rigorous methodology and thoughtful analysis, the authors offer essential insight into these and other key issues concerning the participation of women in the U.S. political system.

Richard A. Seltzer is professor of political science at Howard University. An expert in research methods and the statistical analysis of public opinion, he has studied public attitudes about AIDS, jurors, and racial matters. His recent books include *Mistakes that Social Scientists Make: Error and Redemption in the Research Process* and, with Robert C. Smith, *Race, Class, and Culture: A Study of Afro-American Mass Opinion.* **Jody Newman** is former executive director of the National Women's Political Caucus (NWPC), a national, grassroots organization that is dedicated to increasing the number of women in elected and appointed office. She was political director of the National Women's Campaign Fund from 1983 to 1984 and was manager of Harriett Woods' campaigns for the U.S. Senate in 1982 and 1986. She is the author of *Perception and Reality: A Study Comparing the Success of Men and Women Candidates.* **Melissa Voorhees Leighton** was the membership director at NWPC from 1991–1995.